Ranger Rick's NatureScope

DISCOVERING DESERTS

National Wildlife Federation

LEARNING TRIANGLE PRESS

*Connecting
kids, parents, and teachers
through learning*

An imprint of McGraw-Hill

New York San Francisco Washington, D.C. Auckland Bogotá Caracas
Lisbon London Madrid Mexico City Milan Montreal New Delhi
San Juan Singapore Sydney Tokyo Toronto

Library of Congress Cataloging-in-Publication Data

Discovering deserts/National Wildlife Federation
        p.   cm.—(Ranger Rick's naturescope)
    Includes bibliographical references (p. 88).
    ISBN 0-07-047100-2 (pbk.).
    1. Deserts   I. National Wildlife Federation.
    II. Series.
    GB611.D565   1998
    372.3'57—dc21

                                                            97–36211
                                                            CIP

McGraw-Hill

*A Division of The **McGraw·Hill** Companies*

NATIONAL WILDLIFE FEDERATION®

    2 3 4 5 6 7 8 9 0 JDL/JDL 9 0 3 2 1 0 9 8

NatureScope® was originally conceived by National Wildlife Federation's School Programs Editorial Staff, under the direction of Judy Braus, Editor. Special thanks to all of the Editorial Staff, Scientific, Educational Consultants and Contributors who brought this series of eighteen publications to life.

NATIONAL WILDLIFE FEDERATION EDITORIAL STAFF
Creative Services Manager: Sharon Schiliro
Editor, Ranger Rick® magazine: Gerry Bishop
Director, Classroom-related Programs: Margaret Tunstall
Contributors: Donald M. Silver
Patricia J. Wynne

McGRAW-HILL EDP STAFF
Acquisitions Editor: Judith Terrill-Breuer
Editorial Supervisor: Patricia V. Amoroso
Production Supervisor: Clare Stanley
Designer: York Production Services
Cover Design: David Saylor

McGraw-Hill books are available at special quantity discounts to use as premiums and sales promotions, or for use in corporate training programs. For more information, please write to the Director of Special Sales, McGraw-Hill, 11 West 19th Street, New York, NY 10011. Or contact your local bookstore.

Printed and bound by the John D. Lucas Printing Company.
This book is printed on recycled and acid-free paper.

TM and ® designate trademarks of National Wildlife Federation and are used, under license, by The McGraw-Hill Companies, Inc.

                                                            RRNS

OTHER TITLES IN *RANGER RICK'S NATURESCOPE*

GOAL

Ranger Rick's NatureScope is a creative education series dedicated to inspiring in children an understanding and appreciation of the natural world while developing the skills they will need to make responsible decisions about the environment.

A CLOSE-UP LOOK AT DISCOVERING DESERTS

ooking at the Table of Contents, you can see we've divided *Discovering Deserts* into five main chapters, each dealing with a broad desert theme, followed by a craft section and the Appendix.

Each of the five chapters includes *background information* that explains concepts and vocabulary, *activities* that relate to the chapter theme, and *Copycat Pages* that reinforce many of the concepts in the activities.

You can choose single activity ideas or teach each chapter as a unit. Either way, each activity stands by itself and includes teaching objectives, materials needed, suggested age groups, subjects covered, and a step-by-step explanation of how to do the activity. (The objectives, materials, age groups, and subjects are highlighted in the left-hand margin for easy reference.)

AGE GROUPS

The suggested age groups are:
- Primary (grades K–2)
- Intermediate (grades 3–5)
- Advanced (grades 6–8)

Each chapter begins with primary activities and ends with intermediate or advanced activities. But don't feel bound by the grade levels we suggest. Resourceful teachers, naturalists, parents, and club leaders can adapt most of these activities to fit their particular age group and needs.

OUTDOOR ACTIVITIES

Even if you don't live in a desert area, there are many desert-related activities you can do outside. We've tried to include at least one outdoor activity in each chapter. These are coded in the chapters in which they appear with this symbol:

COPYCAT PAGES

The *Copycat Pages* supplement the activities and include ready-to-copy games, puzzles, coloring pages, worksheets, and mazes. *Answers to all Copycat Pages are on the inside back cover.*

WHAT'S AT THE END

The sixth section, *Crafty Corner,* will give you some art and craft ideas that complement many of the activities in the first five chapters. And the last section, the *Appendix,* is loaded with reference suggestions that include books, films, and desert posters. The Appendix also has desert questions and answers, a desert glossary, and suggestions for where to go for more desert information.

CACTUSES VS CACTI

When we talk about more than one cactus in this issue of *NatureScope,* we use the word *cactuses* instead of the word *cacti*. Both are accepted as plural forms of cactus.

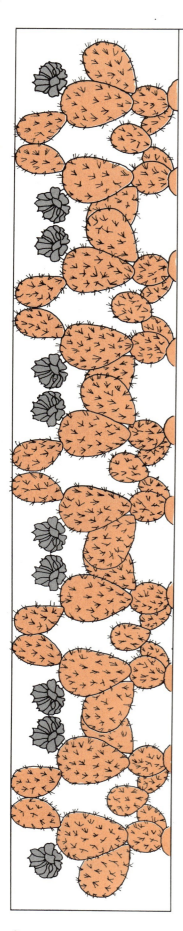

TABLE OF CONTENTS

WHAT MAKES A DESERT A DESERT?

I nch by inch, a grizzled old man crawls along the sand. Sweat is pouring down his face as the sun "cooks" the water from his body. There is not another sign of life anywhere—just sand and more sand. Suddenly the weary traveler sees palm trees on the horizon, and a glimmer of hope dashes through his mind. "Water," he gasps. "Water at last!"

This is the kind of scene many people think about when they hear the word *desert*. But endless stretches of sand typify just one type of desert. Many deserts don't have any sand at all. Instead some are "paved" with smooth pebbles or covered with cracked mud or crystallized salt.

A lot of deserts aren't always hot, either. In fact, many deserts are buried under a cover of snow during part of the year. And deserts are certainly not lifeless. All kinds of plants and animals live in them.

SO WHAT IS A DESERT?

As different from one another as deserts of the world are, they all share one characteristic—they're very dry. Scientists define deserts as areas that get less than 10 inches (25 cm) of rainfall a year and have a very high rate of evaporation. (If the annual evaporation rate of an area is higher than the annual amount of rainfall, the area is considered a desert.) Here are two reasons the evaporation rate in a desert is often so high:

High Temperatures: Most deserts have very little cloud cover. (That's because they lie in zones of high pressure systems. See page 4 for more about high pressure deserts.) Because they have almost no cloud cover, all of the sun's radiation hits the desert floor and reradiates into the air as heat. (In areas with clouds, less of the sun's radiation reaches the earth. The clouds reflect much of the radiation back into the atmosphere.) This large amount of solar radiation heats the desert very quickly and causes the record-breaking high desert temperatures. The hot, dry air causes what little water there is to evaporate very quickly.

Strong Winds: The quick and constant heating of the desert floor causes strong local winds to blow almost constantly in many desert areas. These strong winds greatly increase the rate of evaporation in the desert.

In some deserts in Central Asia, 270 drops of moisture evaporate for every drop that sinks into the ground.

Don't Count on the Rain: Another characteristic of deserts is sporadic rainfall. As we mentioned above, deserts get less than 10 inches (25 cm) of rainfall a year. But if the limited rainfall in deserts fell a little at a time throughout the year, many deserts probably would not look much like deserts. Instead, they'd have a lot more vegetation.

Rain doesn't fall evenly throughout the year in a desert, though. It usually comes in big bursts. In some deserts, none at all may fall for more than a year. And then all of a sudden a huge thunderstorm may dump over 5 inches (12.5

cm) all at once. Most of the water from violent thunderstorms runs off and evaporates before it gets a chance to soak into the soil. That's because a lot of desert soils are made up of very fine particles that fit tightly together and keep the water from soaking in. Water that doesn't soak in quickly evaporates.

Cold Nights, Hot Days: Deserts have some of the most variable temperatures of any places on earth. Because the desert skies are nearly cloudless, the temperatures during the day may sizzle. But without cloud cover to hold in the heat, it radiates into the atmosphere very quickly once the sun goes down. In some deserts, the temperature may drop as much as 77° F (25° C) in 12 hours.

Fantastic and Colorful Landforms: Many desert areas have some of the most spectacular landscapes in the world, from rugged cliffs and painted canyonlands to endless stretches of giant sand dunes. Without the "clutter" of vegetation, the colorful scenery creates bold and dramatic vistas that you can see for miles.

Most desert landforms are shaped by the work of water and wind. Water, often loaded with sand or gravel, races through desert mountains and valleys, grinding out canyons, cutting streambeds, and carving other desert landforms. Desert winds are rock carvers too. They often carry sand grains that scour the desert landscape like invisible sandpaper. With enough sand, the wind can create sand dunes. The sizes and shapes of the dunes depend on the strength of the wind and the amount of sand it carries.

Some of the tallest sand dunes in the world are found in Africa's Sahara Desert. They can be higher than 800 feet (240 m).

WHERE ARE ALL THE DESERTS?

There are about 20 major deserts in the world, spread out on five continents. They cover almost 15% of the earth's land area. That's an area about the size of South America. (See the map on the insert to find out where the world's deserts are located.)

Most of the world's deserts are *hot deserts*. That means they have hot daytime temperatures during most of the year. The Mojave Desert in North America and the Sahara Desert in Africa are two examples of hot deserts.

The rest of the world's deserts are *cold deserts*. For part of the year they have daytime temperatures that often plunge below freezing. Many cold deserts get over half their moisture from snow. The Gobi Desert in Mongolia and the Great Basin Desert in North America are examples of cold deserts that get snow during the winter. (See the insert to find out more about the deserts of the world.)

WHY ARE THE WORLD'S DESERTS WHERE THEY ARE?

High pressure systems, high mountain ranges, and many other conditions cause deserts to form where they do. (Most deserts form because of a combination of conditions.) Here's a look at how the deserts of the world ended up being where they are:

High Pressure Deserts: Many deserts form because they lie in zones of high atmospheric pressure, where dry air is descending. As the descending dry air warms up, it absorbs much of the moisture in the area.

The North and South Poles are very dry because of these descending masses of dry air, as are many desert areas that lie along the Tropic of Cancer (23°N

Latitude) and the Tropic of Capricorn (23°S Latitude). (Because of their cold temperatures all year round, the North and South Poles are usually not considered typical desert areas.) The Sahara Desert, the Australian deserts, and the Arabian Desert are just a few of the high pressure deserts in the world.

Some high pressure deserts are often covered with a damp, chilly fog that forms when cold ocean currents hit warm dry winds. These fog deserts are some of the driest areas on earth. The Namib Desert in southern Africa is an example of a cold fog desert.

The town of Arica, Chile, in the Atacama Fog Desert, gets an average of less than 1/25 of an inch (1 mm) of rain per year. That's the lowest annual rainfall on earth.

Rain Shadow Deserts: When prevailing winds reach a mountain range, they rise quickly and cool, losing most of their moisture as rain. By the time the winds cross over the mountains and sweep down the far side, they are very dry. These dry winds will create a "rain shadow" desert if the area on the far side of the mountains does not get moisture in some other way.

A large desert area in Australia lies in the rain shadow of the Great Dividing Range along Australia's east coast. The Great Basin Desert in the United States is also a rain shadow desert. It lies in the rain shadow of the Cascades and Sierra Nevada Mountain Ranges. The Takla Makan Desert in China and the Patagonian Desert in South America are rain shadow deserts too.

Inland Deserts: Some deserts form because they are just too far from moisture-filled ocean winds. As winds sweep in from the ocean across a large landmass, they rise, cool, and drop their moisture as rain. By the time they reach the center of a large continent, the air can be very dry. (That's why most coastal areas are wetter than inland areas.) The Gobi Desert in Mongolia is a good example of an inland desert. It is so far from the wet ocean winds that by the time the winds have passed through Europe and most of Asia, they have no moisture left.

Evaporation Tricks

Show the effects of evaporation with several quick and easy demonstrations.

Objectives:
Define evaporation. Explain how evaporation affects plants, animals, and landscapes in the desert.

Ages:
Primary and Intermediate

Materials:
- *several buckets of water*
- *sponge*
- *many small pieces of cut-up sponge*
- *ruler*
- *3 shallow pans*
- *salt*
- *stopwatch*
- *chalkboard*

Subject:
Science

ater is "disappearing" or *evaporating* from surfaces all the time. It evaporates from plants, animals, soil, bodies of water, and all other surfaces exposed to the air. In this activity, your group will get a chance to find out how evaporation affects living things in the desert and how it helps shape the way many desert areas look.

WATER AWAY

First show your group how water evaporates. Wipe a damp sponge across a chalkboard. Wait a few seconds, until some dry patches show up. Ask the children where the water went. Explain that the water evaporated—or changed from a liquid to an invisible gas called water vapor. Ask the group to think of other examples of things water evaporates from (wet blacktop in the sun, wet clothes hanging on a line in the sun, and so on).

Next ask the group how heat affects evaporation. Does it speed up the rate of evaporation? Slow it down? Do nothing? (Heat speeds it up.) To show how heat affects the evaporation rate, try these two demonstrations on a sunny day:

- Place a shallow pan in a sunny, open area and an identical pan in a shady area. (Do this in the morning.) Fill the pans with exactly two inches (5 cm) of water. Leave the pans in place all day, then go out at the end of the day and measure the amount of water in each pan. Does one pan now have less water than the other? (There should be less water in the pan that's in the sun because heat speeds up the evaporation rate.) *Note:* You can do this as one big group activity and have everyone go outside to search for the hottest and coolest spots to set the pans. Or you can have the children work in teams, with each group setting out a pair of pans and recording water depth in the morning and afternoon.

- You can show how quickly rainfall evaporates off the hot desert ground with this sidewalk graffiti demonstration. Take the group outside, along with a bucket of water, some pieces of sponge, and a stopwatch. Search for a shady sidewalk (or blacktop) area and a sunny one. Then have the children write their initials on the sunny sidewalk with a damp sponge. Time how long it takes for their letters to evaporate completely. Then do the same thing in the shade. In which area did the water evaporate more quickly? Why? (The initals in the sun should have disappeared faster because of the higher temperature.)

THE EVAPORATION COOL DOWN

Many animals use evaporation "tricks" to help them keep cool in the hot desert. For example, some animals sweat to keep cool. The evaporation of the sweat helps cool the skin. Other animals pant, which allows water to evaporate from their mouths and/or lungs. (Evaporation cools because water is changing from a liquid to a vapor. As this happens, some of the water molecules start moving faster and faster and pull heat from the other molecules. Eventually, some of the molecules change into water vapor, pulling heat away from the surface. The surface is cooled as the water molecules "disappear.")

To show that evaporation cools, take the group outside and bring along a few buckets of water. Have each child roll up his or her sleeves and dip one arm into a bucket of water. (Have them leave the other arm dry.) Now tell them to wave both arms in the air. Ask them which arm feels cooler.

To show the children what happens when salty water evaporates, try this quick and easy demonstration. Dissolve some salt in a shallow pan of water and leave it near a heater or in the sun for two or three days. As the water evaporates, the salt will be left behind. (For more about salt in the desert and how it affects desert plants, see page 53.)

Grit, the Sand Grain

Listen to a short story about the adventures of a sand grain and then draw a desert landscape.

Objectives:
Describe how sand can help wind and water create desert landforms. Draw a picture of a sandy desert scene.

Ages:
Primary and Intermediate

Materials:
- *sand (about two handfuls for each person)*
- *small pieces of sandpaper*
- *drawing paper*
- *chalk*
- *crayons*
- *glue*
- *hand lenses (one for each child if possible)*
- *"Read-to-me" story on page 8*
- *map of the world*
- *paper towels*

Subjects:
Science and Art

Sand is a common feature in many desert areas, including parts of the Sahara Desert in Africa, the Thar Desert in India, the Great Sandy Desert in Australia, and the Gobi Desert in Asia. In all, about 10 to 20% of the world's deserts are covered with sand.

What is sand? Scientists define sand as loose grains of minerals and rocks that are less than 1/12 of an inch (2.1 mm) in diameter, but more than 1/400 of an inch (.06 mm) in diameter. That means that sand grains are smaller than gravel but bigger than silt particles.

In many desert areas, sand helps shape the way desert landscapes look. Sometimes sand is carried by rivers and streams and helps the water grind down rock surfaces, carving canyons, mesas, buttes, and other landforms. (Water can erode rock surfaces without sand, but sand increases the amount of erosion that takes place.) Other times sand is swept about by the wind, abrading rock surfaces and helping to shape the landscape.

In this activity your children can take a closer look at sand and realize that moving sand can grind and carve hard surfaces. First pass out a paper towel to each person and then dump a handful of sand on each towel. Have the children look at the sand closely. (If possible, give each person a hand lens to magnify the sand grains.) Ask what sand is made of. (Sand is usually rock that has been broken down into tiny grains. Rock breaks down from the action of water, wind, and sometimes ice.) Explain that there are many colors of sand because different sands come from different kinds of rocks. (For example, there are white sands made from crumbled white gypsum in some parts of New

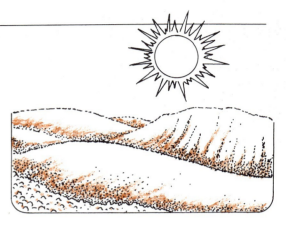

Mexico and black sands made of dark basalt on some Pacific islands.)

Have the children scoop up some sand and rub it between their hands. Ask them how it feels. Then pass out a small piece of sandpaper and a piece of chalk to each person. Have them rub the sandpaper back and forth against the chalk. Ask what happens. Also ask if anyone knows what sandpaper is used for. (It helps grind and smooth rough surfaces on wood and other materials.) Explain that wind or water carrying sand can also grind, just as sandpaper does. For example, during a sandstorm in the desert, the wind may blow hundreds of pounds of sand around at speeds of over 10 miles (16 km) per hour for several days. The sand grains constantly bounce, bump, and grind against all the surfaces they touch. After many, many years, rock surfaces wear down from the constant grinding of the windblown sand.

Now tell the children you are going to read them a short story about what might happen to one grain of sand in the desert. As you read the story, tell the children to think about how it would feel to be a sand grain blown about by the wind and carried along by water.

After the story, ask the children what parts they liked best. Then pass out paper,
(continued next page)

glue, and chalk or crayons. Have each person make a sand "painting" by creating a desert landscape. Have them sketch in their desert scenes with colored chalk or crayons. Then have them glue some sand to areas that might be sandy in their pictures.

BRANCHING OUT

If you live in a desert area, take a walk with the children to look for evidence of wind and/or water erosion on the landscape. Also look for different types of sand that might be present in your area.

If you don't live in a desert area, have your children compare their community to the way a sandy desert looks. Then take a walk in your neighborhood to look for signs of wind or water erosion. Scoop up some of the bottom sediment from a stream to show the children that many moving bodies of water carry sand and other types of debris. The sand helps to erode the streambed and the rocks as it is carried along.

If you live in a sandy coastal community, ask the children how their area is similar to—but also different from—a desert. (For example, it has sand, but is often cooler and wetter than a desert.)

THE ADVENTURES OF GRIT, THE SAND GRAIN

Grit was a tiny grain of sand. He lay in a sand dune in the middle of the Sahara Desert in North Africa. (Ask someone to point out the Sahara Desert on the map.) Grit was just one of billions of sand grains in the Sahara. The sand grains were all a lot alike, but each one was just a little bit different in shape, size, and color.

Grit had been buried in the middle of the same sand dune for over a year. The dune was big—way over 500 feet tall. That's about as tall as 125 kids standing on each other's shoulders!

One day a huge windstorm started to blow across the Sahara. Some of the sand in the dune began to blow away. Suddenly Grit was also lifted into the air. Soon there were thousands of sand grains twirling and swirling in a huge cloud of moving sand. Grit was tossed every which way. He bumped into other sand grains and smacked into rocks. He was dumped on the ground one minute and then swooped up by another gust of wind the next. Again and again he rolled, twisted, and turned. He rubbed against everything—scraping and sliding and scooting along. Once he was in a cloud of sand that swept by a parked car. He and the other sand grains were moving with such force that they scraped most of the paint off the car! Another time Grit and the other grains ground off a lot of a desert palm tree's bark.

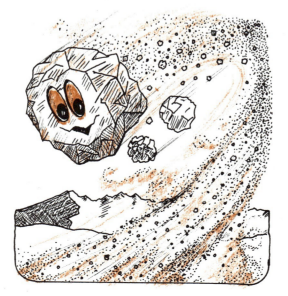

Grit bounced around all afternoon. Up and down and around he sailed, scraping and carving and banging into things. He finally got caught in a high current of air and went sailing over the Mediterranean Sea. (Have someone point out the Mediterranean Sea on the map.) At last he plopped down on a beach—all the way across the sea from Africa. This new place was cool and breezy, not hot and dry as the desert had been. Gentle waves lapped against the shore.

That afternoon a girl walked along the beach and stepped right on Grit. He stuck to her wet foot. As the girl dried off her feet to put on her sandals, Grit ended up clinging to the back of her towel. The girl stuffed her towel (along with Grit) into a waterproof bag and ran off to the hotel where she was staying with her family. In less than an hour, Grit was on a plane headed for the family's home in Tucson, Arizona. (Have someone point out Tucson.)

When the family got home, the girl unpacked her towel and shook it outside. Grit flew off the towel and a gust of wind swept him up once again. Grit bounced along the ground, then finally stopped when he slammed into a cactus. Suddenly, a streak of lightning zigzagged across the sky and thunder rumbled through the valley. The wind blew harder and harder and dark clouds began to pile up in the sky. Raindrops started falling—slowly at first, then faster and faster.

Grit slid into a fast-moving stream that had just formed from all the rain. The stream dragged Grit, along with other sand grains, rocks, gravel, and mud, through a steep canyon. As they all raced along together, they rubbed off tiny pieces of the rocky canyon wall.

As the storm ended Grit was dumped into a huge valley in New Mexico. He lay there for a couple of days until a sidewinder came along and slithered over him. Grit got stuck under one of the snake's belly scales and stayed there as the snake crawled up onto a sand dune. Halfway up the dune, Grit fell off. The wind blew other sand grains into the dune, and soon Grit was covered by a thick layer of sand. After having traveled more than 10,000 miles from his old home in the Sahara Desert, Grit was once again buried deep inside a dune.

Desert Landforms Come to Life

Match clues to pictures of landforms and "act out" desert landform shapes.

Objective:
Describe several types of desert landforms and explain how they form.

Ages:
Intermediate and Advanced

Materials:
- *copies of page 13*
- *copies of the clues on page 10*
- *easel paper*
- *scissors*
- *color pictures of desert landforms (see page 63 in the bibliography for suggestions)*
- *glue*
- *crayons or colored chalk*

Subjects:
Science, Drama, and Vocabulary

Cracked salt flats, deep rock canyons, golden arches, towering sand dunes—all are part of desert landscapes, along with arroyos, playas, buttes, and other landforms. Many of these landforms are carved by fast-moving water and blowing sand. Others form as temporary streams and lakes evaporate, leaving behind minerals, salts, and dried mud.

In this activity, your group can learn about some common desert landforms by matching landform pictures to clues and by playing "landform charades."

PART I: MATCH THE CLUES

First pass out copies of page 13 and copies of the clues on page 10. Also pass out a large sheet of easel paper to each person. Tell the group to cut out the pictures of the landforms and paste them evenly around the edge of the easel paper. Then have them cut out the clue boxes. Tell the group to use dictionaries and

desert reference books to match the clues to the pictures. They should glue each clue box next to the landform it describes. When everyone is done, talk about each of the landforms. Also show the children color pictures of different desert areas. (*Wildlife of the Deserts* by Frederic H. Wagner has some beautiful landform photographs. See page 63 for more information on this book and others that have good desert photos.) Explain that many desert landforms are brightly colored with shades of red, yellow, orange, purple, brown, and white, due to the many different minerals in the rocks. The colors show up more in a desert too, because *(continued next page)* there is so little vegetation covering the ground.

Have the children color in the landform pictures with crayons or colored chalk. Then, in the center of the page, have each person write a poem or paragraph about desert landforms. The poem could be a rhyming poem, a limerick, a haiku, a cinquain, or a free verse poem. (See *NatureScope—Wild About Weather*, Volume 1, Number 3, page 23, for more about haikus and cinquains.) Those who choose to write a paragraph can explain what causes desert landforms to form, describe a desert landscape, or write about a specific landform. Or you could have the children research desert landforms in other countries. (Many of the same landforms have different names in other countries.) Then you can have the children draw a scene in the center of the page showing a desert in another part of the world.

LANDFORM CLUES

butte

1. A constant supply of water, usually coming from underground springs, allows plants and animals to flourish here.

2. When it rains in most deserts, the water usually doesn't flow into oceans or rivers. Instead temporary streams often empty into these dry desert plains or lake beds.

3. The wind "builds" these landforms. Their shapes differ depending on the direction of the wind and the amount of sand in the area.

4. When a river flows through a high, rocky area, it cuts, grinds, and carves the rock year after year and often forms this dramatic desert feature.

5. This unusual landform is often caused when a small hole or crack forms in soft rock and flowing water keeps grinding a bigger and bigger opening.

6. This huge desert landform can be created when hard rock sits on top of softer rock, forming a cap. As wind and water erode the soft rock, steep sloping sides develop. The hard "caprock" forms a flat top.

7. A smaller version of #6, with flat or rounded tops and steep slopes on all sides.

8. These tall landforms are large rock formations that have been worn away at their bases by rushing water. Sometimes harder rocks are left on top, forming caprocks. Also called needles, pedestals, or pinnacles.

9. A dry streambed or gully that has a flat bottom. Is usually smaller than #4, but forms in a similar way. Its name comes from a Spanish word.

PART 2: LANDFORM CHARADES

arch

canyon

After discussing the different types of landforms and how they form, try some "landform charades." Divide the group into three or four teams. Tell each team they need to work together to act out a desert scene using at least two of the landforms on their sheets. (You might want to practice with the whole group first to give them some ideas about how to do this.) Explain that some of the kids in each team can act out landforms, others can be water or sand, and some can be plants or animals. You can have the other teams try to guess which landforms are being acted out, or you can have one person from each team narrate. For example, one group might show how water flows through a canyon and how a playa forms. Some of the kids can be water, some can be the canyon, some can form the playa, and one can be the sun. Each team can dress in desert colors (reds, yellows, oranges, etc.), make props, use sound effects, or put on some special "desert music" while they're acting out their desert scenes.

Landform Clues (answers): 1. oasis 2. playas 3. sand dunes 4. canyon 5. arch 6. mesa 7. butte 8. columns 9. arroyo

Desert Graphics

Make a graph comparing desert climates to other types of climates.

Objectives:
Compare average daily temperatures and rainfall of a desert area and a coastal area. Plot data to make a line graph and a bar graph.

Ages:
Intermediate and Advanced

Materials:
- *copies of page 14*
- *map of the United States*
- *red and black markers*

Subjects:
Science and Math

How do desert climates compare to climates in other areas? Your group can find out by plotting temperature and rainfall data and making a line graph and a bar graph.

First pass out a copy of page 14 to each person. Explain that meteorologists (scientists who study the atmosphere) collect all kinds of weather data, including high and low daily temperatures and average monthly rainfall, from all over the world. You can get a lot of this data by writing to the National Weather Service or by looking in weather almanacs and statistical abstracts.

Have the children look at the data labeled *Average Daily High Temperatures*. Ask if someone can explain what these temperatures mean. (Special thermometers record the highest temperature of the day. Then these daily high temperatures are averaged together for the month.) Now have the children look at the data marked *Average Monthly Rainfall*. The rainfall data for each month was averaged together to get these figures. (If you want your group to learn how to figure average temperatures or rainfall, keep a record of the high and low temperatures and the amount of rainfall in your area. Then have

the children calculate weekly or monthly averages.)

Next have someone point out where Phoenix, Arizona, and Washington, D.C., are located on a map of the United States. Ask the children what type of climate each area has. (Phoenix is located in the Sonoran Desert and has a hot desert climate. Washington, D.C., is near the East Coast and has what is called a humid continental climate.)

Now have the children plot the temperature data from Phoenix with a red marker on the graph marked *Average Daily High Temperatures*. (The first dot is filled in as an example.) Tell them to connect their data dots with a red line. Then have them plot the temperature data from Washington with a black marker and connect the data points with a black line.

Next have them make two bar graphs to compare average monthly rainfalls. One graph should show the average rainfall for Phoenix and the other should show the average rainfall for Washington, D.C.

After the graphing is completed, ask them these questions:
1. In which months was there more than a 20° difference in the average daily high temperatures between Washington and Phoenix? (Jan., Feb., and Dec.)

(continued next page)

2. Which area had the highest average temperature in June? (Phoenix)
3. In which month did Washington, D.C., have over four times the amount of rain that Phoenix had? (All months except Jan. and Dec.)
4. Why do you think data is often plotted on graphs? (The graph creates a "picture" of the information and often makes it easier to understand.)
5. Why is it important to keep records that show the average temperatures and the average amount of rainfall in an area? (It helps farmers predict rainfall and temperatures for the year, it helps scientists keep track of how weather and climate are changing, and it provides a record of what is normal for an area.)

BRANCHING OUT

- Have each person make another line graph, comparing average monthly high temperatures from your area to those in Phoenix, Arizona. Do the same with average monthly rainfall.
- Compare desert climates to other types of climates, such as polar, rain forest, alpine, and grassland climates. Pick cities in each type of climate and then look up the weather data in a statistical abstract or almanac.

- Give the children the following data and have them create their own graphs to compare the average high and low temperatures of Phoenix with those of Washington, D.C.

AVERAGE TEMPERATURES

MONTH	PHOENIX	WASHINGTON
January		
High	65	43
Low	36	28
February		
High	70	46
Low	41	29
March		
High	75	55
Low	45	35
April		
High	83	67
Low	51	46
May		
High	93	76
Low	59	46
June		
High	102	84
Low	67	66
July		
High	105	88
Low	77	69
August		
High	103	86
Low	77	68
September		
High	99	80
Low	69	61
October		
High	88	70
Low	57	50
November		
High	75	57
Low	45	39
December		
High	66	45
Low	38	30

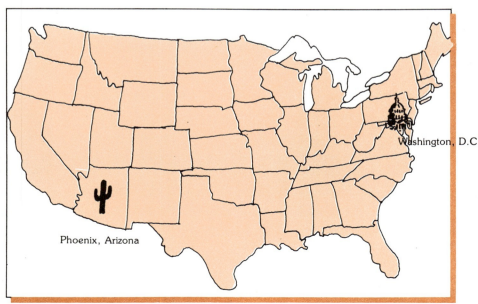

Washington, D.C.

Phoenix, Arizona

COPYCAT PAGE

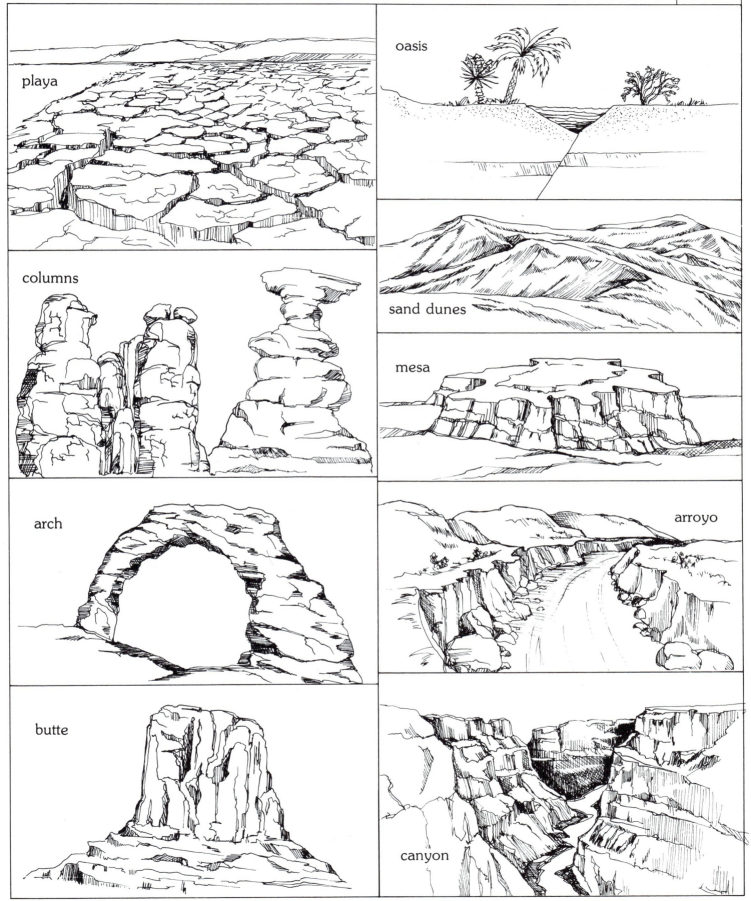

playa

oasis

columns

sand dunes

mesa

arch

arroyo

butte

canyon

AVERAGE DAILY HIGH TEMPERATURES

	PHOENIX, AZ	WASHINGTON, DC
JAN	65	44
FEB	69	46
MAR	75	55
APR	84	67
MAY	93	77
JUN	102	85
JUL	105	88
AUG	102	87
SEP	98	80
OCT	88	70
NOV	75	57
DEC	66	45

AVERAGE MONTHLY RAINFALL

	PHOENIX, AZ	WASHINGTON, DC
JAN	0.7	2.6
FEB	0.6	2.5
MAR	0.8	3.3
APR	0.3	2.9
MAY	0.1	3.7
JUN	0.1	3.5
JUL	0.8	4.0
AUG	1.0	4.7
SEP	0.7	3.0
OCT	0.5	2.7
NOV	0.5	2.9
DEC	0.8	3.0

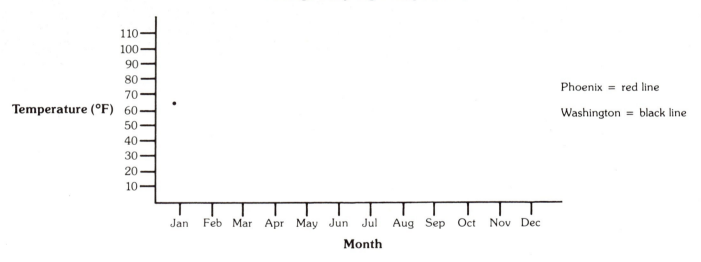

Average Daily High Temperatures

Phoenix = red line

Washington = black line

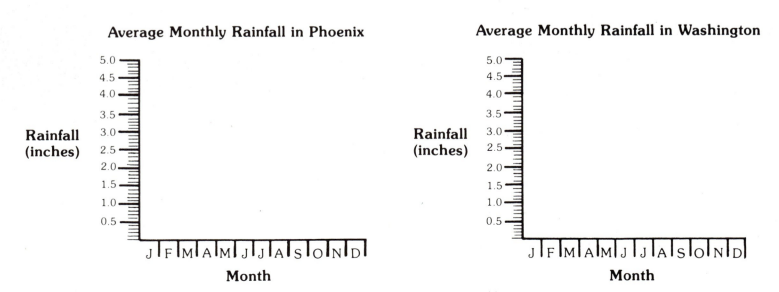

Average Monthly Rainfall in Phoenix

Average Monthly Rainfall in Washington

PLANTS OF THE DESERT

A tiny mustard seed lies buried in the parched clay of the Chihuahuan Desert. No rain has fallen for over a year. But one day in late winter an unexpected shower soaks the ground. The seed soaks up rainwater, and within two weeks it sprouts and blooms under the blazing sun. Thousands of other mustard plants bloom around it, carpeting the desert clay with delicate white flowers. But within a few weeks all of the flowers have withered and died. Behind them they leave a new crop of seeds, specially suited to "waiting out" the long desert dry spells.

These desert wildflowers, like all desert plants, really take advantage of the limited moisture that comes their way. Desert plants also have special ways of dealing with heat and other desert conditions that set them apart from most non-desert plants. Here's a look at some of the ways desert plants are adapted to the desert.

TRANSPIRATION TRICKS

Desert plants, like most plants, use the sun's energy to convert carbon dioxide and water into sugar. During this process, called *photosynthesis,* small pores *(stomata)* on a plant's leaves and stems open to absorb carbon dioxide from the air and to release oxygen (a by-product of photosynthesis). Each time the stomata open, some water is lost. This water-loss process is called *transpiration.*

Losing a large amount of water through transpiration isn't a problem for most plants. They can easily replace the water they lose by sucking up more moisture through their roots. But if desert plants lost a lot of water through transpiration they couldn't replace it as easily and they would die. So they've evolved some special adaptations that help them cut down on this water loss. Here are some of their special water-saving tricks:

Smaller, Fewer, and Deeper: Many desert plants have very small stomata compared to those of other types of plants. They also have *fewer* stomata. And the stomata of many cactuses lie deeper in the plants' tissues than they do in most other plants, which reduces water loss further by keeping the hot dry wind from blowing directly across the stomata.

A Waxy Cover: Plants don't lose water just through their stomata—they also lose some right through the cell walls on their leaves. But the leaves and stems of many desert plants have a thick covering that's coated with a waxy substance. This makes it much harder for water to escape through the leaves' cell walls. (The stomata themselves *aren't* covered with the waxy substance, so they can still open and absorb carbon dioxide.)

Open at Night: Most plants carry out photosynthesis during the day, since that's when the sun shines. And as they photosynthesize, they lose a large amount of water through transpiration because high daytime temperatures cause water to evaporate quickly.

Cactuses also carry out photosynthesis during the day. But unlike most other plants, many of them can transpire at night. These cactuses, and quite a few other desert plants, open their stomata only after the sun goes down and temperatures fall. When the carbon dioxide they need for photosynthesis enters through the pores, the plants store it until daylight. *(continued next page)*

Little Leaves: Many desert plants have small leaves (or no leaves at all). This cuts down on the amount of water a plant loses in transpiration, since a plant with small leaves has less surface area exposed to the sun and wind than it would have if the leaves were larger. Some of these plants carry out most or all of their photosynthesis in their twigs and stems.

Hiding From the Sun: During the hottest part of the day many desert grasses and other plants "roll up" their leaves to reduce the amount of their surface area that's exposed to the sun and wind. Others orient their leaves in such a way that the least amount of surface area is exposed to the sun during the hottest part of the day.

Drop 'em During Drought: Some desert plants grow leaves during the rainy season, then shed them when it becomes dry again. These plants, called *drought-deciduous* plants, photosynthesize through their leaves during wet periods. When drought sets in again and the plants lose their leaves, some of them can photosynthesize through their stems and twigs. And some cut down on water loss even further by shedding their twigs and temporarily shutting down photosynthesis.

A large apple tree loses about 320 quarts (304 liters) of water in a day. A large saguaro cactus, on the other hand, loses less than one glass of water in the same amount of time.

SUCKING IT UP

Besides being able to save some of the water that might otherwise be lost through transpiration, most desert plants are adapted to getting as much water as possible. One way some desert trees and shrubs do this is by growing very deep taproots. Sometimes these roots can get to be more than 100 feet (30 m) long. But the part of the plant that's above ground may stay small for years because the plant puts most of its energy into developing its taproot system.

Many cactuses and desert shrubs have huge, tangled networks of shallow roots that spread out from the plant in all directions. Usually the roots are at least as long as the plant is tall, and they can quickly absorb water from even the slightest rainfall. (Many desert plants have both a deep taproot and a network of shallow roots.)

SHRINKING AND SWELLING

Many desert plants store the water their roots soak up and then use it during drought. Cactuses and a lot of other desert plants—many of which are more than 85% water—store the water in their fleshy leaves and stems. Because they're so "juicy" these plants are called *succulents*.

Some succulents, like the saguaro cactus, have visible pleats or folds that allow them to swell with water during wet periods. The pleats or folds can almost disappear if the plant soaks up a lot of water; then they become visible again as drought sets in and the plant uses the water it's stored.

Many desert plants die to the ground during the hottest part of each year. But the water they've stored in underground roots, tubers, and bulbs sustains them until the next rainy season.

HAIRS, SPINES, AND CHEMICALS

Here are a couple of other "tricks" that desert plants use to stay alive.

Hairy and Prickly: Hairs and spines on the leaves and stems of cactuses and some other desert plants help reduce moisture loss by breaking the wind. They also cast shadows on desert plants, which may protect them from the sun. Sometimes the hairs or spines are shiny and reflect the sun's rays away from the plant. Hairs and spines also protect their owners from hungry animals.

Keeping a Distance: Many scientists think that some desert plants give off chemicals from their leaves or roots that keep other plants from growing nearby. This could help reduce competition for the scarce water supplies.

SEEDS THAT "SLEEP"

Like the desert wildflowers we talked about at the beginning of the chapter, some plants cope with the desert's dryness by not coping at all. During drought they're present only as seeds in the desert soil. For months, years, or sometimes even decades these seeds "wait out" the dry spells in a dormant state. Then, when the right amount of rain falls and soaks into the soil, they sprout and bloom. And when this happens the desert's dry brown landscape can quickly change into colorful fields of wildflowers, herbs, and grasses.

Most of these fast-growing plants don't last very long. Aside from having seeds that are adapted to drought, they have few or no special adaptations to desert conditions. That's why they sprout, flower, and leave behind a new generation of seeds as quickly as possible. Because they're so short-lived, these desert plants are called *ephemerals.*

It wouldn't do ephemerals much good to sprout if there weren't enough water to keep them growing. So the seeds are covered with natural chemicals, called *inhibitors,* that keep them from germinating until enough rain falls. A quick desert shower probably won't wash the inhibitors off a seed, but a real gully washer might—and once the inhibitor has been washed off, the seed can sprout.

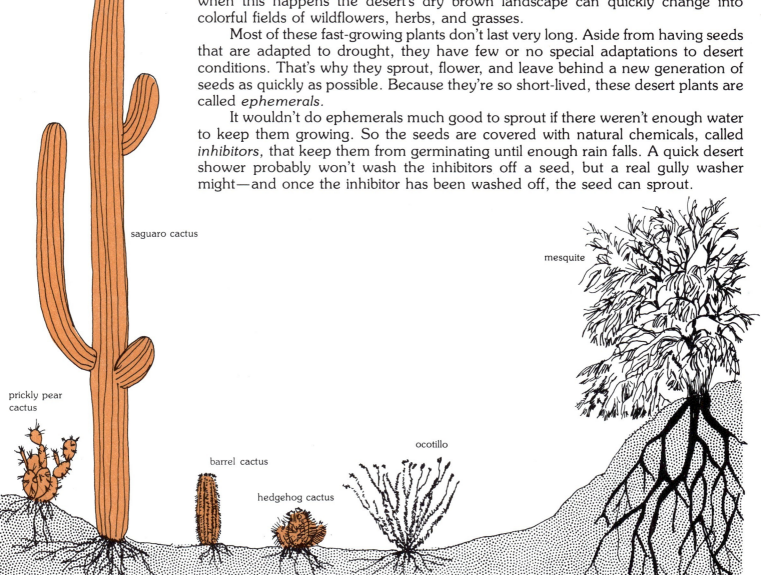

saguaro cactus

mesquite

prickly pear cactus

barrel cactus

hedgehog cactus

ocotillo

Waiting for Rain

Listen to a desert plant story and act out the movements that go with it.

Objectives:
Name one thing all plants need to grow. Talk about how some desert plants "react" to rain.

Ages:
Primary

Materials:
- *"Read-to-me" story provided below*
- *pictures of seeds sprouting*
- *desert plant seeds and materials for growing them (optional)*

Subject:
Science

Have your kids act out a desert story to discover how some desert plants react when rain comes their way. Start the activity by having the kids sit in a circle. Explain that all plants need water to grow. But in the desert plants don't get much water because it doesn't rain very often. When it does rain, it usually pours for awhile, then stops altogether. Many desert plants soak up as much water as they can during and right after these rain showers. Then some of them—especially many of the desert wildflowers—grow and bloom quickly. (See the background information on pages 15-17 for more about how desert plants are adapted to dry conditions.)

A SEED IN THE DESERT

Bruce Norfleet

Once there was a tiny seed. It lay in the sand in a hot, hot desert. The seed needed rain to grow. But every day the hot sun shined down on the tiny seed and no rain fell. (Have the kids hold their hands in front of them in a "sun shape"—see photo.) Then one day the wind started to blow. (Have the kids "blow" like the wind.) The hot sun went behind a cloud. Soon more clouds gathered and covered the sky. (Have them continue to "blow.") They were big, dark storm clouds. And they were full of rain—just what the tiny seed needed! Suddenly lightning flashed and thunder rumbled. Big, fat raindrops started to fall. They started out slowly—*pat, pat, pat.* (Have the kids slowly pat their thighs.)

Next show the kids pictures of sprouting seeds to give them a general idea of the way seeds grow into plants. Tell them they'll be listening to a story about how a seed in the desert grows into a plant and blooms. You might want to go over each of the movements before you read the story, or you can just have the kids imitate the movements as you make them. (The movements are in parentheses within the story.)

After you read the story, you might want to follow up by having the kids plant their own desert wildflowers or cactuses. See "Grow 'em on Your Own" on page 23 for information about ordering seeds and for tips on growing desert plants.

One big drop, and then another, hit the tiny seed. Then the drops started falling faster and faster. (Have them pat their thighs faster and faster.) They pounded down on the tiny seed and the tiny seed became soaked! But soon the rain started to slow down. (Have the kids pat their thighs slowly again.) It got slower and slower and finally . . . it stopped. The hot sun came out again and shined down on the tiny seed, just as it had done before the rain came. (Have the kids hold their hands in a "sun shape.")

But somehow the tiny seed was different now. Soon it started to swell and grow. Then it sprouted! (Have the kids hold their arms in front of them, palms clasped.) A little green shoot grew out of the seed and pushed through the sand. It grew taller and taller each day. (Have the kids slowly raise their clasped hands above their heads.)

Then one day the new plant bloomed! (Have the kids separate their hands and wiggle their fingers.) Many bright yellow flowers covered the plant. And soon the plant would make its own seeds. These seeds would also lie in the desert sand under the hot, hot sun. (Have the kids make a "sun shape.") There they would lie for months or even years, waiting for rain to fall and make them grow.

Cactus Kids

As a group, act out the way a saguaro cactus swells with rain and shrinks during drought.

Objective:
Explain how a saguaro cactus collects and stores water.

Ages:
Primary

Materials:
- *picture of a saguaro cactus*
- *piece of paper*
- *stapler*

Subject:
Science

Here's a fun way to help your group understand how a cactus collects, stores, and uses water.

Before you get started, fold a piece of paper (at least 8½ × 11″) like a fan along the 8½-inch side. The folds should be less than an inch (2.5 cm) wide. Staple the edges of the paper together in several places so that the paper forms a cylinder (see diagram). You'll be using this cylinder later to demonstrate how a saguaro swells as it soaks up water.

Now show the kids a picture of a saguaro (sah-WAH-ro) cactus and tell them that some cactuses, like the saguaro, can store water in times of drought. Explain that even though it doesn't rain very often in the desert, a saguaro is able to collect a lot of rainwater when it *does* rain. That's because it has a huge network of shallow roots that grow away from its trunk in every direction. By growing close to the surface, the roots can soak up a lot of rain quickly—before the sun comes out again and all the rainwater dries up.

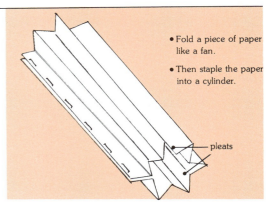

- Fold a piece of paper like a fan.
- Then staple the paper into a cylinder.

pleats

Use a picture of a saguaro to point out the ridges and grooves that make up the cactus's pleats. Show the kids the folded cylinder of paper so they can see more clearly what the pleats of a saguaro look like. Explain that these pleats allow the saguaro to swell and store water. (A 6-ton [5.4-t] saguaro may absorb a ton [.9 t] of water after a rainfall and the trunk may swell a foot [30 cm] or more.) To demonstrate how a saguaro swells, put your hand up through the center of the cylinder. Hold the cylinder straight up and down so that one side is facing the kids. Then press outward with your fingers so that the pleats "unfold" and become less noticeable. Explain that when a saguaro stores water its pleats become less noticeable too. During times when there is no rain, the saguaro uses its stored water—and as it does, the cactus shrinks again. Withdraw your hand from the cylinder and push the pleats back into place to show what the saguaro looks like when it shrinks down again. Tell the kids that the water a saguaro stores can keep it alive through two years of drought.

Now tell the kids that, as a group, they are going to become the trunk of a saguaro and act out what it's like to swell with rainwater and shrink during drought.

Clear a space and have the kids form a big circle. Tell the group to imagine that they're all part of a huge saguaro that's growing right up through the group's center.

Next read "The Saguaro" (left) and go over each of the movements with the kids. After they've had a chance to practice a few times have them try the movements as you read.

THE SAGUARO

I live in the desert
Where the sun brightly shines,
I've got ridges and grooves
And a lot of sharp spines.

Everyone holds hands out in a "sun shape"–see photo on page 18.
Everyone wiggles fingers.

My roots don't grow deep
But they spread far and wide,
To soak up the rain
That I'll store deep inside.

Everyone stretches arms out to the side and wiggles fingers.
Everyone makes slurping sounds.

My body starts swelling
Before the rain stops,
It swells and it swells
As I soak up each drop.

Everyone joins hands and steps backward to form a bigger circle.
Everyone steps backward again to form an even bigger circle.

In times without rain
I get thinner each day,
As I use up the water
That I've stored away.

Everyone steps toward center to make the circle smaller.
Everyone steps toward the center again to make the circle even smaller.

Ice Plants and Elephant Trees

hat do pincushions, sand dollars, and beavertails have in common? They're all names of cactuses! These cactuses, along with a lot of other desert plants, have names that describe what they look like. Your kids can put their imaginations to work in this activity as they learn about some desert plants and their interesting names.

First copy these desert plant names onto a chalkboard or large piece of easel paper: old man cactus, elephant tree, strawberry cactus, teddy bear cholla (CHO-ya), barrel cactus, feather cactus, ice plant, living stones, and pincushion cactus. (Be sure to write or hang the list where all the kids can see it.) Explain that these desert plant names describe the way the plants look. Then pass out drawing paper and crayons, markers, or paints and let the kids use their imaginations to draw what the plants might look like.

When the kids are finished, pass out copies of page 25 so they can see what the plants *really* look like. (Here are the names of some other neat desert plants that you can have the kids draw or research: candle plant, fishhook barrel cactus, ghost flower, panda plant, rabbit brush, rainbow cactus, smoke tree, and yellow bee plant.)

Desert Plants in Trouble

hen most people think of threatened or endangered species, they think of certain kinds of animals. But a lot of plants are also in trouble, and some of the plants that are having the toughest time are ones that grow in the desert. For example, more than 25 cactus species are now on the U.S. Fish and Wildlife Service's list of endangered and threatened plants. Here's a look at some of the reasons many desert plants are disappearing from areas where they once grew:

● Increased tourism and the rising demands for vacation homes, retirement communities, and other housing areas have prompted the development of desert land. For example, many cities in the southwestern United States are expanding. Every year more and more roads and buildings crop up in desert areas surrounding cities.

● People who drive dune buggies, motorcycles, Jeeps, and other off-road vehicles (ORVs) can run over and destroy a lot of desert plants. They can also rip up desert soil and raise huge dust clouds. Once the desert soil has been degraded by ORVs, it often can't support the plants that used to grow in it.

● Cattle and sheep often are allowed to overgraze desert grasses and other plants. With fewer plants to hold the desert soil, it erodes away. This makes it difficult or even impossible for the original plant species to grow back. Instead, certain "undesirable" plants sometimes grow in their place.

● Strip mining destroys desert plants and also "strips off" several layers of desert soil. Native plants usually can't grow back in desert areas that have been strip mined.

- Desert land irrigated for agricultural use is no longer available for desert plants. And irrigation itself can eventually ruin desert soil for crops *and* desert plants. That's because irrigation water can "draw up" salts that naturally occur in desert soils. The salt concentrates in the topsoil and makes it too salty to support either crops or the native desert plants that once grew there. Such land is often abandoned and left barren. (See page 46 for more about salt in the desert.)

- In many desert areas tourists illegally dig up cactuses for souvenirs.

- Vandals illegally cut open cactuses, carve their initials in them, or chop off parts of their stems. Some people even use cactuses for target practice.

- Cactus "rustlers" illegally dig up plants and sell them for landscaping or ornamental use. Cactuses are very popular with property owners in the southwestern U.S. who want drought resistant plants for landscaping. They're also popular with collectors in many other parts of the world.

- Digging up large desert plants for landscaping or destroying them because they're considered undesirable is often

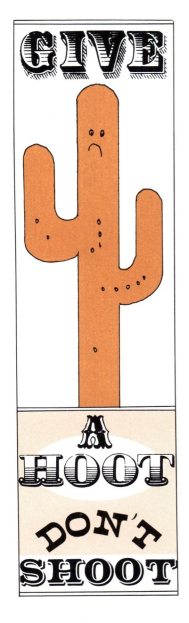

harmful to other plants nearby, to animals in the area, and to desert soil. For example, many desert plants need shade when they're young and can't survive when their "shade trees" are removed. And many animals that eat or live in desert plants are left without a food supply or a home. Also, desert soil left exposed by the removal of desert plants can eventually erode away.

Review some of these problems with your group. Then tell them that things *are* being done to help desert plants. For example, areas such as Saguaro National Monument, Organ Pipe Cactus National Monument, and Joshua Tree National Monument have been set aside to protect desert plants and their habitats. Many states have also passed laws to protect their native desert plant species. And those plants on the Fish and Wildlife Service's list of endangered and threatened species are protected by both federal and international law. But unfortunately these measures are not effective enough.

Explain that the laws in some states are not as strict as they are in other states, so some desert plants aren't as well protected as they could be. And many of the existing state and federal laws are hard to enforce, especially with small staffs and limited budgets. Officials have to patrol thousands of square miles looking for thieves and vandals, and "rustled" cactuses are hard (and sometimes even impossible) to distinguish from cactuses grown in greenhouses. Also, protection of endangered animals is often given priority over that of endangered plants, so the plants have been neglected in many cases.

Ask the kids why desert plants are important. (Their roots help bind the soil to prevent erosion, and they provide food, shade, and shelter for many desert animals.) Then have the kids pretend they're agents for a "Desert Plant Protection Society." Their job is to design posters that will advertise one of the problems desert plants face. To do this they must come up with a slogan and then illustrate it. See the drawings for some examples of slogans and pictures you can suggest to get the kids started.

Close-Up Comparisons

Compare cactuses to woodland plants.

Objectives:
Describe two ways cactuses are adapted to the desert. Discuss two differences between cactuses and woodland plants.

Ages:
Intermediate and Advanced

Materials:
- *cactuses (one per group)*
- *woodland plants such as ferns and ivies (one per group)*
- *newspaper*
- *flashlights (one per group)*
- *plastic bags*
- *pieces of string (for closing the plastic bags)*
- *petroleum jelly*
- *sponges (one per group)*
- *plastic margarine tubs (2 per group)*
- *scissors*

Subject:
Science

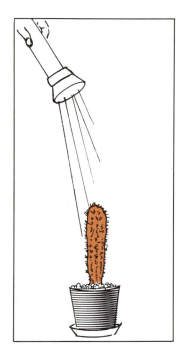

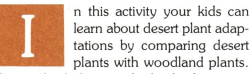n this activity your kids can learn about desert plant adaptations by comparing desert plants with woodland plants. To get the kids started, divide them into groups of three or four. Give each group one of the desert plants and one of the woodland plants. Be sure to buy only cactuses that have been grown from seed. Cactus "rustlers" often make a lot of money by illegally digging up and selling wild cactuses—some of which are listed as endangered species. (For more about cactus rustling, see "Desert Plants in Trouble" on page 20.) It's also better to buy—rather than dig up—the woodland plants you'll be using. (Most areas have laws against collecting certain wild plants and many are very hard to keep alive.)

Warn the kids to handle their cactuses *very carefully!* They should *never* pick up a cactus with their bare hands—instead, have them handle their cactuses with rolled newspaper. (Don't have them use gloves. Spines can get stuck in the fabric and then work their way into the wearer's skin.) Keep a pair of tweezers handy in case you have to remove some spines.

SPINY SUN SHADES

Have the kids try this comparison to see how shape and spines can reduce the amount of sun that reaches a plant.

Pass out one flashlight to each group. Then turn out the lights and have the kids shine their flashlights onto their woodland plants from above. Point out the fact that the leaves of each plant "catch" a lot of the flashlight's beam, just as they catch sunlight. Now have them shine the flashlights onto their cactuses from above. Do they notice any difference between how much of the woodland plant was illuminated and how much of the cactus is in the flashlight's beam? Explain that the more flattened sideways or barrel-shaped the cactus is, the less light will fall on the plant as a whole—especially light from directly overhead. In the desert, when the sun is directly overhead at the hottest part of the day, a cactus that's flattened laterally (sideways) or shaped like a cylinder gets very little direct sunlight on its stem.

Now have the kids shine the flashlights on their cactuses from different angles. (Make sure they don't hold the flashlights too close to the plants—shadows won't show up well if they do.) No matter which angle they choose they should see that the spines cast shadows onto the trunk. (These spines shade the plant to keep it from being scorched by the hot desert sun.)

BAG A PLANT

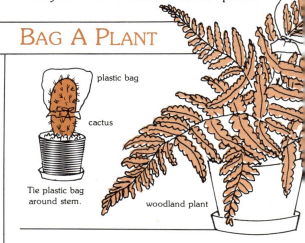

plastic bag

cactus

Tie plastic bag around stem.

woodland plant

Plants lose water through their leaves and stems when they photosynthesize. This water loss process is called transpiration. (See page 15 for more about transpiration.) Discuss transpiration with your group and then let them see this process in action in both desert and woodland plants as you do this demonstration.

Use a fairly large cactus and a large woodland plant. Put a plastic bag over a stem or over the top of the cactus and tie the bag closed with a piece of string. Then put a plastic bag over a leafy branch on the woodland plant. Put the plants near a sunny window or in a sunny spot outside. After awhile small droplets of water should condense on the insides of the bags. Tell the kids that this water is coming from each plant as it transpires. Ask them which of the two plants transpired more. They should notice that there's much more condensed water on the plastic bag enclosing the woodland plant.

A SEAL OF WAX

Desert plants have many ways of reducing the amount of water they lose through transpiration (see page 15). One way they do this is by having thick leaves and stems with waxy coatings. This comparison will show the kids that a covering can help reduce water loss.

If the plants aren't too spiny let the kids feel and compare the leaves and stems of the two plants. Then give each group a dry sponge, two margarine tubs, and some petroleum jelly and have them follow these steps:

1. Pour ¼ cup (60 ml) of water into each tub.
2. Cut the sponge in half. (Both pieces should be exactly the same size, so make sure the kids measure.)
3. Cover one side and all four edges of one piece of sponge with a thin layer of petroleum jelly. Then lay it in one of the margarine tubs on its *ungreased* side.
4. Lay the other piece of sponge in the other margarine tub.
5. Watch as the sponges soak up the water. Then keep track of how long it takes for the sponges to dry out.

The ungreased sponge should dry out first. (It'll take about three or four days.) Explain that the petroleum jelly acts like the wax that covers some cactuses and prevents water from evaporating quickly.

BRANCHING OUT

● Have your kids make a cactus dish garden or a cactus terrarium. For suggestions on how to set these up, see *The Prickly Plant Book* by Sue Tarsky, *The Terrarium Book* by Charles M. Evans, and *The Complete Book of Terrarium Gardening* by Jack Kramer.

plastic bag

Grow 'em on Your Own

Grow desert wildflowers and cactuses from seeds and graph their growth rates.

Objectives:
Recognize differences in the growth rates of different desert plants. Describe the life cycle of a desert ephemeral.

Ages:
Primary, Intermediate, and Advanced

Materials:
● *desert wildflower and cactus seeds (see end of activity for how to order)*
● *plastic seed trays*
● *potting soil*
● *perlite*
● *aquarium gravel (very fine)*
● *sand*
● *gravel (coarse)*
(continued next page)

Let your kids compare the growth rates of two different kinds of desert plants by growing both kinds from seed. You may be able to get everything you'll need from a garden supply shop. (Some stores may sell cactus seeds, but these usually are available only in mixes. You can use these mixes if you want, but you may not know which species you are growing. You can also order seeds by mail. For addresses of suppliers, see the end of the activity.)

To start, first discuss the life cycle of a desert ephemeral plant and also review some of the adaptations that help cactuses survive. (See pages 15-17.) Then divide the group into smaller groups of four to six kids. Give each group some wildflower and cactus seeds, two seed trays, some gravel, and a soil mixture containing one part sand, one part perlite, and one part potting soil. (Be sure to use sand and soil from the store—beach sand is much too

salty and soil from your backyard is not sterile. Check to see if the store carries premixed soil for cactuses—the kids can use this instead of the soil/sand/perlite mixture.)

Then have the kids plant their seeds by following these directions:

SOWING THE SEEDS

Cactus seeds
1. Poke a lot of small drainage holes in the bottom of a clean dry seed tray.
2. Place ½ inch (1.25 cm) of coarse gravel in the bottom of the seed tray.
3. Fill the seed tray with the soil mixture to about ½ inch (1.25 cm) from the top. *Do not* pack it tightly.
4. Place the cactus seeds on top of the soil, about ¼ inch (6.25 mm) apart. Don't press them into the soil—just sprinkle a small amount of soil mixture (about the thickness of the seeds) over the seeds. *(continued next page)*

- clear plastic bags
  (1 for each tray)
- rubber bands
- plastic seed labels
- graph paper
- rulers with metric
  increments

Subjects:
Science and Math

5. Put the tray in a sink filled with about 1½ inches (3.75 cm) of water. Let it soak until the soil is moist (about one minute).

6. Cover the soil with a thin layer of very fine aquarium gravel (just enough to cover the soil).

7. Push two small seed labels down into the soil, on opposite sides of the tray. The seed labels should stick up about 2 inches (5 cm). Then put the tray into one of the plastic bags and seal the bag with one of the rubber bands. (The seed labels should keep the plastic bag away from the soil so that none of the seedlings will touch it.)

8. Put the tray in a place that's always at least 70° F (21° C) and has indirect light.

9. Once the seeds have sprouted, open the bag to let air circulate. When the seedlings have spines, remove the tray from the plastic bag.

Wildflower Seeds
1. Follow steps #1-6 for cactus seeds.
2. Put the tray in a sunny place that's always at least 70° F (21° C).

Special Tips
- If the soil in the cactus or wildflower seed tray starts to get dry, place the tray in a sink filled with 1½ inches (3.75 cm) of water until the soil is moist again.
- If a lot of water condenses on the inside of the plastic bags, remove the cactus seed tray and put it in a clean, dry bag. (see step #7)
- If fungus starts to grow on the soil surface, scrape if off with a seed label. Then transfer each of the cactuses to a pot filled with soil and gravel as in steps #1-3.
- If the cactus seedlings turn very light green, place them in a spot where they will get some direct sunlight.
- It's easy to kill cactuses by overwatering them. Check the cactus soil for moisture by pushing the sharpened end of a pencil into it. If the pencil wood feels at all moist, don't water the cactus.

GRAPHING THE GROWTH

It will take about one to two weeks for both the cactus seeds and the wildflower seeds to sprout. As the kids watch the plants grow, have them measure and graph the changes in the plants' heights. (Younger children may not be able to measure and graph accurately, but they can still have fun growing the plants.) The cactuses will grow quickly at first but then will grow more slowly and won't get very tall, so have the kids measure them with metric rulers every other day. The wildflowers will grow more quickly so the kids should be able to see some changes if they measure them every day.

When you are finished observing the plants and graphing their growth, let each child take one home. They can transplant each plant into a small pot. The pot should have a ½-inch (1.25-cm) layer of coarse gravel on the bottom and should contain 1-2 inches (2.5-5 cm) of the soil mixture. (Use a seed label to gently dig up each plant and its roots, and then place it in a hole near the side of the pot. Fill in around the base of the plant with extra soil mixture and pack lightly.)

You might want to recommend *The Prickly Plant Book* by Sue Tarsky to help the kids care for their cactuses.

WHERE TO GET SEEDS

To order cactus seeds write to the Desert Botanical Garden, Gift Shop, 1201 North Galvin Pkwy., Phoenix, AZ 85005. Saguaro seeds and cactus seed mixes are available. (For more about cactus supplies, see page 64.) You can also order desert wildflower seeds such as gold poppies, desert marigolds, and mixes of different species.

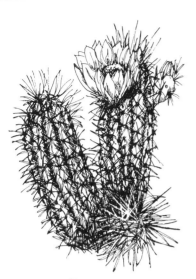

Barrel Cactus
The spines of some barrel cactuses were used by Indians for fishhooks.

Strawberry Cactus
These cactuses have strawberrylike fruit that are covered with spines.

Teddy Bear Cholla
If you touch this tree, watch out—small, prickly branches may fall off it and stick into your clothes or skin.

Living Stones
These plants look like pebbles and sometimes they blend right in with the real rocks around them.

Elephant Tree
During long dry spells, this tree can save water by dropping its leaves.

Feather Cactus
The spines on this plant form feathery clusters.

Old Man Cactus
The white hairs that cover this plant help protect it from the sun.

Pincushion Cactus
Many of these cactuses don't grow to be more than 2-3 inches (5-7.5 cm) tall.

Ice Plant
The water stored close to the outside surface of this plant's leaves and stems looks like small beads of ice.

ANIMALS OF THE DESERT

I magine going through life without ever taking a drink of water. Or living without air conditioning in a place where summer temperatures climb to more than 117° F (47° C). If you were a kangaroo rat you'd probably do both, because your natural habitat would be the desert. Like other desert animals, you'd have plenty of adaptations that would help you deal with two desert problems: scarce water supplies and high temperatures.

ADAPTING TO DRYNESS

Drinking What You Eat: Some desert animals, such as pack rats, "drink" by eating juicy cactuses and other plants that contain a lot of water. And some, such as many snakes, get all the moisture they need from the mice and other small animals they eat.

Kangaroo rats, pocket mice, jerboas, and gerbils manage to get a lot of moisture from their main diet of dry seeds. Some kangaroo rats, for example, store seeds in their burrows. The air in the burrows is humid, and the seeds soak up some of the air's moisture. So when a rat eats the seeds it's stored, it also gets the moisture that the seeds have soaked up. It can also chemically manufacture water, called *metabolic water,* from dry seeds as they are being digested. (Many other desert animals can satisfy part of their water needs with metabolic water too.)

Moving On: Like desert rodents and other small desert animals, large desert dwellers can get some of their water from the food they eat. But to get all the moisture they need, most of these bigger animals have to *drink* water too. So in order to find ponds, rivers, and other sources of water, many types of large desert animals sometimes wander great distances. For example, in the course of a year, some Asian and African desert antelope and other desert animals may wander hundreds of miles, from water hole to water hole.

Drinking Fog: In some deserts the only source of water is the fog that rolls in from the coast. Some of the animals that live in these deserts have special ways of taking advantage of their foggy surroundings. For example, in the Namib, a fog desert in Africa, certain species of darkling beetles perch on the tops of dunes with their abdomens pointing upward. Fog moving in from the coast condenses on their cool bodies and trickles down into their mouths. Some desert snakes, lizards, and other animals can also drink moisture that condenses on their bodies.

Thirsty Babies: Raising young puts an extra water demand on desert mammals, birds, and other animals that take care of their offspring. Like all mammals, desert mammals can supply moisture to their offspring with milk from their own bodies. But most birds must bring water to their nestlings—usually in the form of juicy insects. (A few birds, such as doves, regurgitate liquids from their crops into their youngsters' mouths.)

The desert birds known as sandgrouse have a unique way of supplying their chicks with water. After drinking at a water hole, an adult male submerges its breast feathers in the water. These feathers are especially designed to soak up and hold moisture. When the sandgrouse is "filled up," it flies back to its young. The chicks poke at the feathers with their beaks and slurp down the liquid.

When the Time Is Right: Some desert animals can escape drought. They do this by "sleeping" through dry times in much the same way as some non-desert animals hibernate through the winter. This dry weather "sleep" is called *estivation.*

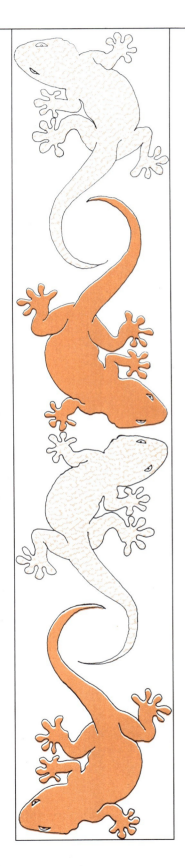

Spadefoot toads are well known desert estivators. They "wait out" dry periods in underground burrows for months or even years, covered with a jellylike substance that keeps them moist. Vibrations caused by heavy raindrops hitting the ground wake up the toads. Then they quickly dig to the surface, find a mate, and lay eggs in the temporary pools created by the rain. Soon they return underground. The tadpoles that hatch from the eggs must grow quickly, before the pools dry up. But not all of them make it to adulthood in time—and many of the ones that don't survive become meals for scavengers. The ones that do manage to survive crawl out of the pools as adult toads and dig their own burrows.

Certain desert rodents, snails, and spiders estivate through the hottest and driest times of the year. Scientists think that it's scarce food—not so much drought or other factors—that triggers this hot weather "sleep." (Plants and other sources of food tend to die back when it's really hot and dry.) So by estivating, animals can avoid not only hot, dry conditions but also a food shortage.

Saving Water Through Kidney Power: One of the ways some desert animals can keep from drying out is by "saving" water that would otherwise be used to make wastes. For example, kangaroo rats have efficient kidneys that use as little water as possible to produce urine. Not using much water produces a urine that is much more concentrated than that of most non-desert animals.

BEATING THE HEAT

Staying Out of the Sun: Many desert animals avoid the burning daytime heat by foraging at night. Others are active only in the cool morning and late afternoon. But in the middle of the day, when ground temperatures can rise to 190° F (88° C), most desert animals find a place to rest out of the scorching sun. Rodents, lizards, snakes, and insects dive into cool, humid burrows, dig down into the sand, or crawl under rocks. Other animals look for shade under bushes and trees—or wherever they can find it. And some birds, such as hawks, eagles, and vultures, soar high above the earth, where temperatures are much cooler.

Keeping Fat in Its Place: All animals need some fat, since fat is an important energy reserve in "lean" times. But a layer of fat keeps heat from leaving the body. To keep from retaining any more heat than they have to, a lot of desert animals concentrate their fat supplies in certain areas. This strategy leaves them with plenty of "fat-free" areas for heat escape.

A camel's humps are a good example of a fat storage area. (It was once thought that the humps stored water.) And the fat-tailed gecko and fat-tailed mouse both are desert animals named for the area where they store their fat.

Big Ears and Long Legs: Jackrabbits, jerboas, and fennec foxes aren't related—but these desert animals and several others all have one outstanding feature in common: big ears. Oversized ears do more than pick up sound waves. They also help to cool their owners by radiating heat. Blood vessels in the ears are located just under the skin, and as air flows around them it cools the blood. The cooled blood circulates through the rest of the body, picking up more heat to carry to the ears for "disposal."

Like big ears, the long legs of the camel and gazelle radiate body heat. And long legs also keep vital internal organs away from the hot ground. Ants, beetles, and lizards keep their insides cooler by straightening out their legs as they walk across the hot sand.

Desert Relay Race

Imitate the movements of desert animals in a relay race.

Objectives:
Describe three desert animals and the ways they move. Talk about some of the ways these animals are adapted to the desert.

Ages:
Primary and Intermediate

Materials:
- **pictures of a sidewinder rattlesnake, a golden mole, a camel, a kangaroo, and a web-footed gecko**
- **string or some other material for marking relay race boundaries**

Subjects:
Science and Physical Education

By competing in a desert relay race, your kids can learn about some of the ways desert animals are adapted to their special habitats. Begin by talking about each of the animals listed below. Show a picture of each animal as you explain how it moves, then let the kids try out the movements before the actual race begins.

Sidewinder: The sidewinder, a kind of rattlesnake, lives in open, sandy areas. Most snakes have a hard time getting a grip on a sandy surface, but the sidewinder has "solved" this problem by moving in a special way. True to its name, this snake moves over the sand sideways. It uses its strong muscles to loop its body to the side in a constantly moving S-curve. The rough scales on its undersides dig into the sand, helping it to move surprisingly fast. And since only two points of its body touch the hot sand at any one time, the snake stays cooler.

To imitate a sidewinder, the kids can lie on their sides, facing the direction they want to go. Have them move by first sliding the upper halves of their bodies along the ground, then their legs and feet. (If the kids get too tired in this lap of the race, have them "sidewind" only to the ending line. Then they can get up and run back to the starting point.)

Golden Mole: This small, sand-colored animal is streamlined for burrowing. It's shaped like a torpedo and has short, broad forelimbs for "swimming," breast stroke style, through the sandy desert soil. As it moves underground, its shovel-shaped nose pushes sand and soil out of the animal's way. Have the kids "run" on their knees and move their arms in breast stroke motions to imitate a golden mole.

Camel: Camels walk with a swaying gait, moving both legs on one side of their bodies at the same time and then both legs on the other side. A camel's broad feet—each as big around as a dinner plate—keep the animal from sinking into the soft sand. The soles of the feet are covered with leathery skin that protects them from hot sand and sharp rocks.

Two children can work together to imitate the camel's walk. Have one of the children stand behind the other and put his or her hands on the other child's shoulders. Then have the kids move by stepping forward with their right feet, then their left feet, and so on. (They'll be moving both legs on one side at the same time.)

Kangaroo: The kangaroo uses its strong hind legs to bound away from enemies in a series of zigzag jumps. Other desert animals, such as the kangaroo rat and jerboa, also have very strong hind legs for jumping and zigzagging. Scientists think that this type of movement helps some animals escape from predators. (Most deserts don't have a lot of thick vegetation that animals can hide in.)

The kangaroo is easy for kids to imitate—just have the kids in your group hold their arms close to their chests while they jump forward.

Web-footed Gecko: The web-footed gecko, a type of lizard, gets its name from the webbing between its toes. This special feature helps the gecko run on soft sand without sinking in and also helps the animal scoop out sand when it's digging a burrow. To run the gecko lap of the race, the kids can drop to their hands and knees and move quickly on all fours.

After talking about these desert animals and having the kids practice the movements of each one, divide the group into teams of six. Then set up the relay course by marking a starting line and an ending line (about 25 feet [7.5 m] away) with string.

Next line up the teams behind the starting line. Let the kids know what animal each of them will be imitating by calling out the animals in the order they'll be "run." (Remember that *two* children are needed to imitate a camel.) Then give the starting signal. Have the first runners race to the ending line, then back to the starting line. They must touch the next person in their particular line to start the second lap of the race. The first team to run all the laps of the race is the winner.

Sunrise, Sunset

Make a day and night wheel to show when desert animals are active.

Objectives:
Define the words diurnal and nocturnal. Name three desert animals that are diurnal and three that are nocturnal.

Ages:
Primary and Intermediate

Materials:
- *copies of pages 32 and 33*
- *lightweight cardboard*
- *construction paper*
- *crayons or markers*
- *small, pointed scissors*
- *glue*
- *2 thermometers*
- *soil*
- *sand*

Subjects:
Science and Crafts

Have your kids make a desert "day and night" wheel to learn about some of the desert animals that are active during the day and about others that are active at night.

Begin by telling the kids what the words *diurnal* and *nocturnal* mean. Explain that diurnal animals are active mostly during the day, whereas nocturnal animals are active mostly at night. Point out that many animals are nocturnal, then ask the kids if they can think of any examples. (bats, crickets, flying squirrels, opossums, owls, raccoons, many small rodents such as mice, and so on) Explain that being active when it's dark is one way to keep from being seen by hungry predators.

In the desert, being active at night is also one way to avoid the scorching daytime temperatures. Even most diurnal desert animals find a shady place to rest when the sun reaches its midday peak.

After talking about diurnal and nocturnal animals, pass out copies of pages 32 and 33 to everyone. Then have the kids put their wheels together by following the instructions below.

HOW TO MAKE A DESERT DAY AND NIGHT WHEEL

1. Color the cactuses and other plants on sheet A.
2. Color the day and night skies on sheet B. Also color the animals.
3. Glue sheet A to a piece of construction paper. Glue sheet B to a piece of thin cardboard. Then cut out both circles along the solid lines.

4. On circle A, cut out the large window and the four smaller windows.
5. Place circle A on top of circle B, then push a paper fastener through the centers of both circles.

When everyone's finished, show the kids how to "work" their wheels. Have them move the top circle until the sun fills the large window. The animals that appear in the four smaller windows are diurnal animals. Most of them are active only in the early morning and late afternoon. They rest quietly in the middle of the day, when the temperatures are hottest. Next have the kids turn their wheels to the night sky, making the nocturnal desert dwellers come into view.

Now talk about each of the diurnal and nocturnal animals on the wheel, using the information on the next page.

(continued next page)

DIURNAL DESERT ANIMALS

Leonard Lee Rue III jackrabbit

- **Desert Iguana**—Can tolerate higher temperatures than many other animals can. Often active in the heat of the day, when other animals are resting quietly in the shade. Sometimes digs holes in the sand, which it crawls into to escape the heat.

- **Ground Squirrel**—Feeds in the early morning and late afternoon, returning frequently to its burrow to cool off. Remains underground during the hottest hours of the day.

- **Jackrabbit**—Does not burrow, but uses the shade of a tree or bush as shelter from the hot sun. Its big ears release heat. (For background information on heat radiation, see page 27.)

- **Roadrunner**—Finds shade wherever it can during the heat of the day. Pants to give off body heat.

NOCTURNAL DESERT ANIMALS

- **Elf Owl**—Roosts in abandoned woodpecker holes during the day. Hunts at night.
- **Kit Fox**—Stays in den during day. Pants to cool off and also radiates heat from large ears.
- **Pack Rat**—Is active only at night. Spends day in nest. Sometimes hauls pieces of juicy cactus into its nest and then rips the pieces open to expose the moisture they contain. As the moisture evaporates, it helps cool the nest.
- **Scorpion**—Spends day in burrow. Hunts at night, paralyzing insects, small mammals, and other prey with the stinger on its tail.

BRANCHING OUT: A DEMONSTRATION

On the desert's surface, the temperature can soar to 190° F (88° C)—but just a few feet underground, it may be 60° F cooler. Kangaroo rats, kit foxes, rattlesnakes, scorpions, and a host of other desert animals take advantage of this temperature difference: To beat the midday heat, they retreat to burrows and dens beneath the hot surface.

Try this demonstration to show your kids how an underground "retreat" can help desert animals escape high temperatures. Sometime in the early afternoon, bury a thermometer a few inches beneath the surface of the ground. Lay another thermometer right on the ground. An hour or so later, have the kids dig up the first thermometer. While they're digging, tell them to touch the soil itself to feel how cool it is. Then have them compare the temperature reading of the underground thermometer with that of the surface thermometer. They should notice a difference of several degrees or more. You can repeat this demonstration in sand to show an even more dramatic difference in temperatures.

Animal Match-Up

**Play a game to match
desert animals with their
adaptations.**

Objective:
*Describe four desert
animals and some of
their adaptations to
desert life.*

Ages:
*Intermediate and
Advanced*

Materials:
- *reference books*
- *copies of page 43*
- *drawing paper*
- *crayons or markers*
- *slips of paper*

Subjects:
Science and Art

By playing this match-up game, your kids can take a look at some desert animal "parts" and behaviors to see how they work together to create an animal that's adapted to desert life. Here's how to play:

Divide your group into teams of three or four and make a set of the adaptation clues (listed below) for each team, copying each clue onto a separate slip of paper. (Don't include the names of the animals on the slips.) Then mix up the order of each set of clues and pass out a set to each team. Also give each team member a copy of page 43.

Using reference books and the Copycat Page, the teams must figure out which three clues fit one of the animals pictured on the Copycat Page. The object of the game is to be the first team to correctly fit the clues to the animals they describe. (You might want to add a little excitement to the game by setting a time limit.)

When the game's over, talk about the six animals and their adaptations. Look on page 42 for some information that you can use in your discussion.

ANIMAL ADAPTATION CLUES

Kangaroo Rat:
- My hind legs help me jump straight up into the air, out of danger's way.
- I eat a lot of seeds and never need to take a drink of water.
- I use my long tail for balance when I jump.

Fringe-Toed Lizard:
- Scales that stick out on the sides of my toes keep me from sinking into sand.
- My shovel-shaped nose helps me dig a path when I dive under the sand.
- Special scales keep sand out of my eyes.

Roadrunner:
- My dark skin absorbs the sun's warming rays.
- I'd rather run than fly.
- I catch rattlesnakes to eat by stabbing at them with my beak.

Spadefoot Toad:
- A sharp ridge on each of my hind feet helps me dig underground.
- Even though I'm a desert animal, I can't reproduce without a lot of water.
- I sleep through the driest times of the year.

Jackrabbit:
- I can get all the water I need from the plants I eat.
- I can "gallop" at speeds of up to 40 miles (64 km) per hour.
- My big ears give off a lot of body heat and help to keep me from overheating.

Scorpion:
- I capture insects and other small prey with my large claws.
- One sting from my tail, and my prey can't move a muscle.
- If I'm a female, I carry my young on my back.

BRANCHING OUT: IMAGINARY ANIMALS

Here's a creative way to wind up a discussion of desert animals and their adaptations. Give each person three of the adaptation clues from the activity. Then have everyone create an imaginary desert animal using his or her three clues. The kids should decide what their particular animals look like, how they get their food and water, how they escape predators, how they beat the desert heat, and anything else they want to focus on. Have them draw pictures of their "new" desert animals in their habitats, then have each person present his or her animal to the rest of the group.

NAME OF DESERT	TYPE	LOCATION AND SIZE	REASON DESERT FORMED	PHYSICAL FEATURES	EXAMPLES OF PLANTS AND ANIMALS	SPECIAL FACTS
PATAGONIAN 16	C	• Argentina • 153,000 mi² (398,000 km²)	[mountain symbol]	• covered by stony and sandy areas	• cactuses, grasses, shrubs • Patagonian fox, Patagonian hare, puma, rhea	• Sea lions and penguins live along the coast of this desert. • similar to the Great Basin Desert in size and physical appearance
SAHARA 17	H	• northern Africa • 3.5 million mi² (9.1 million km²)	[sun symbol]	• covered by mountains, rocky areas, gravel plains, salt flats, huge areas of dunes • areas in the central Sahara sometimes get no rain for years at a time	• acacia, grasses, tamarisks • addax antelope, dorcas gazelle, fennec fox, horned viper, jackal, jerboa, sandgrouse, spiny-tailed lizard	• largest desert in the world • fewer than 2 million inhabitants (mostly nomads such as the Tuareg) • crossed by Arab caravans since the 10th century
SONORAN 18	H	• southwestern United States (Arizona, California) and parts of Mexico (Baja Peninsula, Sonora) • 120,000 mi² (312,000 km²)	[mountain symbol]	• covered by sand, soil, and gravelly pavement • gets more rain than any other North American desert	• agave, Coulter's globemallow, creosote bush, desert Mariposa lily, mesquite, ocotillo, paloverde, saguaro • coati, elf owl, Gila monster, kangaroo rat, pack rat, roadrunner, sidewinder, tarantula	• most complex animal-plant community of any desert • one of the most beautiful deserts in the world
TAKLA MAKAN 19	C	• western China • 600,000 mi² (1.6 million km²)	[I / mountain symbol]	• covered by sand dunes and rocky soil	• grasses, shrubs • Bactrian camel, jerboa, long-eared hedgehog, gazelle	• The word "Takla Makan" means "place from which there is no return." • crossed by Marco Polo in the 13th century
THAR 20	H	• India and Pakistan • 77,000 mi² (200,000 km²)	[sun symbol]	• majority of desert covered by sand dunes; rest covered by gravel plains	• acacia, euphorbias, grasses, shrubs • black buck, dromedary camel, great Indian bustard, Indian spiny-tailed	• small villages of ten to twenty houses scattered through the Thar

Deserts Of The World

NAME OF DESERT	TYPE	LOCATION AND SIZE	REASON DESERT FORMED	PHYSICAL FEATURES	EXAMPLES OF PLANTS AND ANIMALS	SPECIAL FACTS
ARABIAN 1	(H)	• Arabian Peninsula • 900,000 mi² (2.3 million km²)	☀	• covered almost entirely by sand; has some of the most extensive stretches of sand dunes in the world	• acacia, oleander, saltbush • desert locust, dromedary camel, gazelle, jackal, lizards, oryx	• Nomadic Bedouin tribes have travelled through the Arabian Desert for thousands of years.
ATACAMA 2	(C) ≋	• coasts of Peru and Chile • 54,000 mi² (140,000 km²)	⋀⋀⋀ ☀	• covered by sand dunes and pebbles • one of the driest areas on earth	• bunchgrass, cardon cactus, tamaruga trees • lizards, llama, Peruvian fox; nesting area for many seabirds	• Only a few thousand people (mostly farmers) live in the inland desert areas. • large deposits of sodium nitrate found in this desert (sodium nitrate is used to make gunpowder)
AUSTRALIAN (Great Sandy, Victoria, Simpson, Gibson, and Sturt) 3 — 7	(H)	• Australia • these five deserts cover more than one third of Australia—that's over 890,000 mi² (2.3 million km²)	(I) ☀ Gibson and Sturt also ⋀⋀	• Great Sandy, Victoria, and Simpson are sandy; Gibson and Sturt are stony	• acacia, casuarina tree, eucalyptus, saltbush, spinifex grass • blue-tongued lizard, dingo, fat-tailed mouse, kangaroo, marsupial mole, rabbit-eared bandicoot, sand goanna, spinifex hopping mouse, thorny devil	• Aborigines have lived in the Australian deserts for over 30,000 years.
CHIHUAHUAN 8	(H)	• north central Mexico and southwestern United States (Arizona, New Mexico, Texas) • 175,000 mi² (455,000 km²)	☀	• high plateau covered by stony areas and sandy soil • many mountains and mesas	• cactuses, Chihuahuan flax, creosote bush, lechuguilla, mesquite, Mexican gold poppy • coyote, diamondback rattlesnake, javelina, kangaroo rat, roadrunner	• largest North American desert • Big Bend National Park located here; more species of birds seen in Big Bend than in any other National Park in the United States

#	Desert	Climate	Location	Area	Terrain / Soil	Plants	Animals	Notes
9		C	and southern Mongolia	450,000 mi² (1.2 million km²)	(I) soil and areas of small stones called "gobi"	grasses	Bactrian camel, gazelle, gerbil, jerboa, lizards, onager, wolf	Khan in the early 13th century; many nomads now settling on government-run farms
10	GREAT BASIN	C	western United States (Idaho, Nevada, Oregon, Utah)	158,000 mi² (411,000 km²)	covered by sand, gravel, and clay; many mountain ranges, basins, and large expanses of salt flats	greasewood, sagebrush, shadscale	bighorn sheep, jackrabbit, pocket mouse, poor-will, pronghorn antelope, sage thrasher, side-blotched lizard	Great Salt Lake located here
11	IRANIAN	C	Iran, Afghanistan, and Pakistan	150,000 mi² (390,000 km²)	covered by coarse gray soil, stony pavement, and salt flats	grasses, pistachio trees, shrubs	monitor lizard, onager, oryx, scorpion	world's largest salt flat located here
12	KALAHARI	H	southwestern Africa	200,000 mi² (520,000 km²)	covered by sand dunes and gravel plains	acacia, aloe, baobab tree, tamarisk tree	gazelle, gerbil, ground squirrel, hyena, jackal, sandgrouse, springbok	Bushmen have lived in the Kalahari for 20,000 years.
13	MOJAVE	H	southwestern United States (Arizona, California, Nevada)	25,000 mi² (65,000 km²)	covered by sandy soil, gravelly pavement, and salt flats	creosote bush, desert sand verbena, Joshua tree, mesquite	bighorn sheep, chuckwalla, coyote, jackrabbit, sidewinder, zebra-tailed lizard	Death Valley located in this desert
14	MONTE	H	Argentina	125,000 mi² (325,000 km²)	covered by sand and soil	cardon cactus, creosote bush, paloverde	armadillo, cavy, jaguarundi, puma, tinamou, tuco-tuco	very similar to the Sonoran Desert
15	NAMIB	C	coast of southwestern Africa	52,000 mi² (135,000 km²)	covered by sand dunes along the coast and gravel farther inland	aloe, bunchgrass, lichens, welwitschia	darkling beetle, fringe-toed lizard, golden mole, jackal, sidewinder viper, web-footed gecko	coast of the Namib Desert is world's greatest source of gemstones

(C)

- parts of the Middle East and southwestern Soviet Union

- 215,000 mi² (559,000 km²)

(I) ⋀⋀⋀

- covered mostly by extensive stretches of sand dunes

- alhagi shrub, saxaul tree, sedges, thick ground cover

- crossed by caravans following silk route from China to Europe in ancient times

- desert tortoise, gazelle, gerbil, saiga antelope

- The great city of Samarkand, once a cultural and religious center of central Asia, was located here.

KEY TO DESERT CHART

REASON DESERT FORMED   TYPE OF DESERT

⋀⋀⋀ ☀ = rain shadow

= high pressure system

(I) = inland

(H) = hot desert

(C) = cold desert

= special type of cold desert, covered with a cool fog during much of the year; fog caused by cold ocean currents

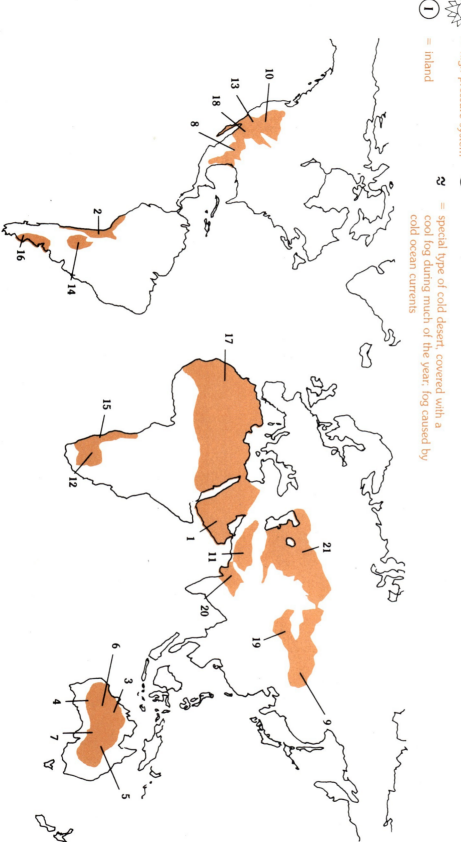

DESERT COMMUNITIES

 desert cockroach scurries across one side of a sand dune. Suddenly a fringe-toed lizard lunges from behind a yucca plant and snatches the cockroach in its jaws. Running on feet built like snowshoes—great for moving in sand—the lizard disappears with its prey behind the yucca.

On the far side of the dune a snake winds its way downward, erasing the tracks a desert kit fox made before dawn. A pale desert grasshopper leaps out of the snake's path and lands a few feet away. The grasshopper blends in so well with the pale brown sand that it seems to disappear. Overhead a turkey vulture sails on rising warm air as it searches for a meal of rotting flesh.

Cooler night temperatures bring even more activity. A tiny white yucca moth flutters in the desert moonlight. Her body is bloated with eggs as she lands on a sticky stamen inside a yucca blossom. She will pollinate the blossom and then lay her eggs inside the fertilized pistil. When her eggs hatch, the caterpillars will feed on some of the seeds that form.

As the moth flies off, a nighthawk swoops down and snatches her from the air. Nearby a kangaroo rat peers out of its sandy burrow and then creeps out to search for seeds. It scoots back to its burrow when it hears the loud cry of a nearby coyote.

In this sand dune community, the plants and animals interact in many ways—just as plants and animals do in all types of communities. Predators chase prey, and prey use all kinds of "tricks" to try to escape. Plants provide animals with food, water, and shelter, and animals help plants with pollination and seed dispersal.

UNRELATED LOOK-ALIKES

If you visited every desert in the world, you'd find that many plants and animals from different deserts look similar or behave in similar ways. For example, jackrabbits in North America have huge ears. And so do bat-eared foxes that live in southern and eastern African deserts. These animals are unrelated, but both have adapted to harsh desert conditions in a similar way: Their big ears help them keep cool. (See page 27 for more about adaptations that help desert animals deal with high temperatures.)

Scientists who have studied habitats around the world have found that plants and animals that live in similar types of environments often "find the same solutions" to similar problems by evolving in similar ways. This is called *convergent evolution.* Here are some other examples of convergent evolution found in deserts:

- Patagonian hares (which are actually a type of rodent and not a hare at all), jackrabbits, and many other desert animals have adapted to living in areas with very little vegetation by evolving special ways to move. Many jump and zigzag across open areas to escape from predators.
- Many desert plants in non-related families have developed sharp thorns, spikes, and needles, such as cactuses in North America and acacia trees in Africa. This feature discourages animals from eating them.
- Sidewinders of North America and sand vipers of Africa have evolved the same efficient way of moving through sand. Both throw their bodies out to the side and "loop" their way across the sand.
- Many euphorbias in Africa store water in their stems, just as the cactuses of North and South America do.

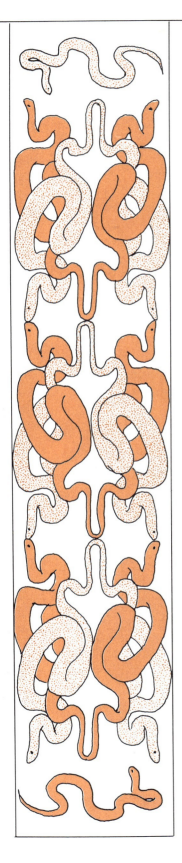

VARIED AND FRAGILE

Although desert communities are similar to other communities in the types of relationships the plants and animals form, they are unique in several ways. Faced with intense heat, a high evaporation rate, and sporadic rainfall, the plants and animals of the desert have evolved many specialized adaptations and behaviors that help them stay alive in the harsh environment. (See pages 15-17 and 26-27 in chapters 2 and 3 for more about plant and animal adaptations.)

Desert communities are also varied. Although deserts are usually very hot and dry, the soil types, amounts of rainfall, landforms, altitudes, and weather patterns vary greatly from one desert to the next and even within the same desert. These physical differences create different kinds of plant communities, which in turn support different kinds of animal communities. For example, soil and weather conditions in some parts of the Sonoran Desert support a thriving community of saguaro cactuses, organ pipe cactuses, and many other succulents. These plants provide food, water, and shelter for elf owls, white-winged doves, jackrabbits, pack rats, cactus bugs, roadrunners, Gila woodpeckers, peccaries, and many other desert creatures. Farther north in the Great Basin Desert, soil and climate conditions are very different. The Great Basin Desert is a cold desert, with fewer plants and almost no succulents. Sagebrush and saltbush are two of the most common plants. Sagebrush lizards, sage sparrows, sagebrush voles, and sage thrashers are some of the animals adapted to living in the sagebrush community.

Deserts are second only to rain forests in the variety of plant and animal species that live there.

Deserts are also different from other communities in another way—they are more fragile than most other types of habitats. One reason is that many of the plants and animals in the desert grow very slowly due to the harsh conditions— especially the lack of water. For example, it may take 20 years for a saguaro cactus to grow a foot, or 15 years for a desert tortoise to reach maturity. This means that it can take a long, long time to replace a loss when a plant or animal dies.

The desert is also so hot and dry that decomposition is a very slow process. When something dies, it takes a long time for it to break down and be recycled back into the soil. And that means it takes a long time to replenish nutrients and minerals in the soil. This slow decomposition also causes litter and other people-made damage to last for generations.

In many desert areas, habitat recovery is also a very slow process because of the dry air. For example, in California you can still see the tread marks made by the tires of army tanks over 50 years ago. And the damage done by a motorcycle race in 1973 will probably last more than a century! (See the background in Chapter 5 for more about desert problems and people.)

In some desert areas, an orange peel takes seven years to decompose!

A Desert Variety Show

Lights. Music. Action! "Ladies and Gentlemen, it's time for the *Discovering Deserts Variety Show,* featuring the Cactus Comedy Review, the Pollination Pals, the Scavenger Squad, the Nitty Gritty Sand Band, and much, much more." In this "show biz" activity your group can research different aspects of desert communities and use music, dance, and skits to dramatize what they've learned.

Before organizing the show, briefly discuss desert community life and talk about some of the topics the children might want to cover in the variety show. Explain that even though deserts have very harsh conditions, desert animals and plants form the same relationships with each other as animals and plants do in other communities. (See pages 34 and 35.)

Divide the group into teams and explain that each team will be responsible for coming up with some kind of act based on a desert-related topic. For example, some of the teams could think up acts based on plant and animal relationships (parasite-host, predator-prey, pollination, scavengers, etc.). Others could focus on convergent evolution (see page 34), desert landforms (see page 9), how desert communities differ around the world, or something about deserts and people (see page 45). Then assign each team a general desert-related topic or let them pick a topic on their own.

The acts the kids come up with should be fairly short (no longer than 10 minutes), and should include a part for each person on the team. Each act should also teach the other members of the group something about desert life. Tell the kids they can write a group poem, put on a funny skit, sing a song, act out a short drama, read a group story, make up a dance, or do anything else that would be entertaining as well as educational. Then give them time to research their topics. (See "A Sample Desert Variety Show," below, for some ideas for acts.)

After the groups have decided what kind of act they want to do, have them discuss their ideas with you to make sure they're on the right track. Then have them write out the parts. Give the teams time to rehearse their acts and also provide them with materials so they can make any props, stage scenes, or costumes they might need. (See page 58 for directions on how to build a giant paper-mache saguaro cactus. You might want to have several of the children build a few of these cactuses to help "set the stage." Or one of the groups might be able to use a cactus in their act.)

Once the teams have their acts ready, you can have all the kids put on the show for each other. Or you can stage a more formal production in front of other children and adults. Either way, the children will have a chance to show off, in a creative way, what they've learned about deserts.

SAMPLE DESERT VARIETY SHOW

Act I: The Cactus Comedy Review

Sally Saguaro: Good evening, folks. My name is Sally Saguaro and this is my side kick, Ollie Organ Pipe. Does anyone know what we are? Right, cactuses.

Ollie: Yeah. We're just two wild and crazy cactus kids.

Sally: Don't mind him, folks. He's been in the sun too long.

Ollie: Hey, Sally.

Sally: Yeah, Ollie?

Ollie: What do you get if you cross a prickly pear cactus with a peanut butter sandwich?

Sally: I don't know, what?

Ollie: A sandwich that really sticks to the roof of your mouth!

(*Stage notes:* Each time a punch line is given, someone can carry a big sign behind Sally and Ollie that says either LAUGH or BOO.)

Sally: That was pretty dumb, Ollie. Now

I've got one for you. What makes desert animals fall asleep?

Ollie: Your jokes.

Sally: No, silly. The sandman.

Ollie: Not bad, not bad. OK, what do you call two cactus look-alikes?

Sally: I give up.

Ollie: A Prickly Pear.

(This skit can continue with a few more desert jokes and maybe a silly poem about cactuses or desert life from a cactus's point of view.)

Act II: The Nitty Gritty Sand Band

Samuel Sand Grain: Good evening, folks. My name is Samuel Sand Grain and this is my family—Shelly Sand Grain, Sharon Sand Grain, Susie Sand Grain, Steven Sand Grain, and Sheldon Sand Grain. We all came from the same piece of sandstone. And we've just come back from a singing tour in the Gobi Desert.

Shelly Sand Grain: Tonight we'd like to perform two of our favorite hits—in fact they've just hit rock-bottom on the charts. Ready to grind them out, guys? A one and a two and a three and a four . . .

(Sing to the tune of "I've Been Working on the Railroad.")

We've been grinding in the valley,
Up and down the desert land.
We've been grinding in the valley,
Making rocks crumble into sand.

Can't you hear the wind a blowin'
Throughout the night and day.
Can't you hear the sand grains grinding,
Eroding the rocks away.

Steven Sand Grain: Our next song is one you can all join in on. You might have heard it before. It's called "10 Billion Grains of Sand in the Dune." Here we go!

(Sing to the tune of "100 Bottles of Beer on the Wall.")

Verse I:
Ten billion grains of sand in the dune
Ten billion grains of sand
The wind comes in and blows us around
Nine billion grains of sand in the dune

Verse II:
Nine billion grains of sand in the dune
Nine billion grains of sand
The wind comes in and blows us around
Eight billion grains of sand in the dune . . .
and so on.

Act III: The Scavenger Squad

(*Stage notes:* The vultures could wear stockings over their heads and black capes to imitate the bald heads and dark bodies of vultures. The beetles and flies could wear hats with antennae made out of wire.)

Vulture I: We don't get much respect.

Vulture II: Yeah, it's a dirty job. But someone's got to do it.

Fly: Without us, the desert would be overflowing with dead bodies.

(Then have them recite this chant. You can divide up the parts or have them all say it together.)

We're the scavengers.
Yeah, we're the scavengers.
We search the deserts high and low
We look for rotting meat, you know.
We're the scavengers.
Yeah, we're the scavengers.

We vultures soar in the desert sky
Until a carcass catches our eye.
We're the scavengers.
Yeah, we're the scavengers.

We beetles and flies are on the prowl
For animal bodies, rotten and foul.
We're the scavengers.
Yeah, we're the scavengers.

We keep the desert clean and neat,
As we gobble up decaying meat.
We're the scavengers.
Yeah, we're the scavengers.

OTHER IDEAS:

- Present a short segment of a desert soap opera called Evaporation Place or The Edge of the Desert. Include information about real animals and plants of the desert.
- Present a short skit about cactus rustling, starring the C-Team as the "good guys" who capture the rustlers.
- Make up a dance called the Predator Shuffle, featuring Germaine and Michael Jackal.
- Make up a group poem about the yucca and the yucca moth and how they help each other survive in the desert.

The Desert Scramble

Play a running game to learn about competition in the desert.

Objectives:
Explain what competition is. Discuss limited resources and how they can affect desert communities.

Ages:
Primary and Intermediate

Materials:
- *construction paper*
- *markers*
- *straight pins*
- *pictures of a coyote, bobcat, ringtail, and jackrabbit*

Subjects:
Science and Physical Education

In many desert areas, finding a drink can be tough. That's because water is often very scarce. Here's an active way for your kids to find out what it's like to compete for limited water in the desert while trying to avoid being eaten by a predator.

Start off the activity by talking about competition. Ask someone to explain what competition is. Then ask if anyone can think of an example of how people compete with each other. (competition in sports, competition for grades, competition for a music award, and so on) Explain that animals often compete with each other, but it's not quite the same as competition between people. Animals (and people) compete with each other for food, water, shelter, and living space—the four things all animals need to survive. But unlike humans, animals never *think* about trying to "beat out" other animals for something. They are driven to compete only by an instinct to stay alive and reproduce.

Now explain that in many desert communities, as in many other types of communities, the resources can be limited. For example, there may be a short supply of water or limited amounts of food or available nesting sites. Ask how that would affect the animals that live in the desert. (A desert area could support only a certain number of animals, depending on its resources.) Now tell the children they will be playing a running game outside to see how a limited resource limits the number of animals that can live in one place.

Before going outside, assign each child a part to play. Explain that six of the children will be jackrabbits, six will be ringtails, four will be water holes, three will be coyotes, two will be bobcats, and one will be the sun. (Adjust the numbers to fit the number of children in your group.) Have each person write what he or she is on a piece of construction paper. (Make sure the kids write in big, easy-to-read letters.) Pin the papers to the kids' backs.

Next talk about each part. Explain that ringtails and jackrabbits are two animals that live in the desert and need to drink water. (Many desert animals get the water they need from the food they eat.) Coyotes are predators that often eat jackrabbits, as well as other small mammals, birds, and reptiles. (Coyotes also eat insects, carrion, and fruit.) Bobcats are predators that eat ringtails, jackrabbits, and other small mammals, as well as birds and reptiles. (If possible show the children a picture of each animal.) Also explain that the kids who are water holes will represent water for the desert animals and the person who is the sun will represent the hot, dry conditions in the desert that cause water to evaporate quickly.

Now take the group outside. Mark the game's boundaries, making sure that the game area is big enough for a lot of kids to run around in. To play the "Desert Scramble" have the children spread out, forming a huge circle. (Make sure the kids leave a lot of space between each other.) Explain that the object of the game for each person depends on what part that person is playing. For example, when you say go, the object for the jackrabbits and the ringtails is to tag a water hole before getting tagged by a predator. The object for the coyote is to tag a jackrabbit. The object for the bobcat is to tag a ringtail or a jackrabbit. (Explain that coyotes and bobcats also need water, but for the purposes of this game they cannot tag a water hole.) The object for the sun is to tag a water hole before all are tagged by jackrabbits or ringtails. And the object for the water holes is to avoid being tagged.

Once someone is tagged, both the tagger and the person tagged must go and "sit out" the rest of the round. After everyone has been tagged that can be tagged, see how many ringtails and jackrabbits were able to find a water hole. Were some left without water? Were others eaten before they had a chance to get a drink? Explain that in this game water was the main limiting resource, or *limiting factor,* that determined the number of ringtails and jackrabbits the area could support. Play the game several times and let the kids switch roles.

The Desert Daily Times

Write articles for a desert newspaper.

Objectives:
Write a newspaper article or special feature about some aspect of desert life. Describe how a newspaper is arranged.

Ages:
Intermediate and Advanced

Materials:
- *paper and pencils*
- *reference books*
- *markers*
- *paste or glue*
- *large sheets of construction paper*
- *sample newspapers*
- *hole puncher*
- *yarn*

Subjects:
Science, Writing, Geography, Social Studies, and Art

Have your group learn more about desert communities, as well as discover what's in a newspaper, by creating their own desert newspaper. From desert obituaries to travel to local news, the *Desert Daily Times* can have it all!

First pass out a copy of a local newspaper to every two or three children. (If possible, give all of them the same day's newspaper.) Go through the newspaper, page by page, and discuss how it is arranged. Point out the major features and sections. (Different papers are divided and arranged in different ways.) Then explain to the group that everyone will be working together to produce a desert newspaper. Each person will have to come up with a story idea, a news item, or an idea for some other newspaper feature.

Have the children work in small groups to think up the contents of one section of the paper. For example, you might have three or four children covering national news and another group of children covering local news. Each group should work together, but each person should be responsible for one article, story, comic strip or cartoon, puzzle, obituary, or other feature of the paper. Explain what a by-line is and tell the kids that each person will have a by-line on his or her contribution to the paper.

Tell the kids to include as many desert facts as possible, but to make their stories or features entertaining too. Encourage them to write from an animal or plant's point of view or to present deserts in a unique way. (See the ideas listed below.) You could also have the group mix fun articles with more serious ones for variety.

After each group is finished, paste the articles, stories, comic strips, and other features to large sheets of construction paper. Then punch holes in the paper and tie it together with yarn. Read some of the articles out loud and discuss them (or have the children read their own contributions). Then leave the paper out for everyone to flip through when they have some free time.

SOME SAMPLE IDEAS FOR THE DESERT DAILY TIMES

- Obituary: *Sam Saguaro Was Found Shot to Death Early Tuesday Morning—Vandals Suspected of the Crime!* (Can talk about how saguaros are in trouble from being shot at as well as from off-road vehicle damage and cactus rustling. See "Desert Plants in Trouble" on page 20.)
- National News: *Penelope Pupfish Is in Big Trouble.* (Can talk about why some kinds of pupfish are endangered and how other desert animals are also having a hard time surviving.)
- Local News: *Willie Pack Rat and His Friends Are Having a "Burrow" Sale at 1212 Saguaro Cactus Lane.* (Can talk about the things Willie collects and the creatures that live in a pack rat burrow.)

- Local News: *Elton Elf Owl Moves Into New Apartment and Says View Is Great!* (Can explain how Gila Woodpecker moved out of a saguaro hole and how Elton moved in, what his apartment looks like, what he eats, and so on.)
- Local News: *New Arrivals Come to Town.* (Can talk about how the last rainstorm brought some new color to the neighborhood as the ephemerals bloomed. Can explain what ephemerals are and why they bloom only at certain times of the year. See page 17.)
- Travel: *Sandy Sand Grain Blows In After Journey to the Patagonian Desert.* (Sandy could talk about what she saw on her trip. She could also describe a sandstorm or discuss erosion.)

(continued next page)

- World News: *The Bustards Are Coming, The Bustards Are Coming!* (Can talk about how bustards and other animals in the desert migrate when conditions get too harsh. See page 26.)
- Classified Ads: *Burrow — Almost New — Great Location — Close to Food and Shade — Call 825-HOLE.* (Can also list other desert items that might be found in a desert classified section.)
- Editorial: *Deserts on the Move.* (Can talk about how deserts are spreading. Could be told from the point of view of

a creosote bush or some desert animal. See page 52.)
- Weather: *New Record Set in Death Valley — No Rain for 628 Days.* (Can talk about the weather or the climate in deserts around the world or just in North America.)

Other categories that might fit into the *Desert Daily Times* include sports, business, crossword puzzles, word scrambles, people, TV or radio, style, advice columns, and food.

Community Squares

Cut out desert plant and animal squares and paste them onto a desert scene.

Objectives:
Describe three plant and animal relationships that exist in the Sonoran Desert. Explain how plants and animals in a community depend on the non-living environment.

Ages:
Intermediate and Advanced

Materials:
- *copies of pages 43 and 44*
- *easel paper*
- *glue*
- *crayons or chalk*
- *rulers*
- *scissors*
- *reference books (see page 63 for suggestions)*
- *map of the United States*
- *pictures of desert communities*

Subject:
Science

In spite of the harsh conditions, desert communities support a wide variety of plant and animal life. In this activity, your group can compare desert communities around the world and then focus on the varied life of the Sonoran Desert in North America. They will see that the plants and animals in all communities depend on each other and on the non-living parts of the environment to survive.

First ask the children to think about desert communities around the world. List some of the plants and animals that live in desert communities. (Some examples are camels, roadrunners, cactuses, tumbleweeds, lizards, mountain lions, kangaroos, Joshua trees, sidewinders, jackals, and desert locusts.) Then show the children some pictures of different deserts and point out the variety of plants and animals that live in each one.

After they look at pictures of various desert communities, ask the children to list some of the ways deserts of the world look different from one another. (Some have sandy soil, some have rocky soil, some are buried in snow during part of the year, some are covered with fog, some have canyons and mesas, others are covered with salt flats or sand dunes, and so on.) Explain that these physical differences provide special growing conditions that support certain kinds of plants. The plants, in turn, support certain kinds of animals.

Next write the word "plants" on the board. Make a list of the things plants need in order to survive. (sunlight, water, special types of soil, animals and wind to pollinate their flowers and spread their seeds, the right type of climate, protection from animals that eat them, and so on) Then write the word "animals" on the board and make a list of the things animals need in order to survive. (plants for food and shelter, water, a place to make their homes, the right kind of climate, other animals for food, minerals and vitamins, and so on)

Now pass out copies of pages 43 and 44 to each person. Explain that the plants and animals shown on the pages live in the Sonoran Desert. (Have someone point to the Sonoran Desert on a map.) Give the children some research time to find out as much information as they can about the plants and animals shown on the pages, and also about the Sonoran Desert in general. They should find out what the animals eat, how they depend on the plants, where the plants live, and how the plants and animals depend on the non-living parts of the environment (soil, sunlight, and water). As they do their research, have them color in the plant and animal pictures.

After the kids have completed their research, pass out a large sheet of easel paper to each person. Provide crayons, glue, and scissors for the group. Tell the children to draw a scene of the Sonoran Desert, using the information they have gathered about what it looks like. (Later they'll fill in the scenes with pictures from their Copycat Pages.) Point out that even though the Sonoran Desert is considered one big desert, it contains many different types of habitats, such as sandy plains, river canyons, dry streambeds, rocky washes, silt-covered bajadas at the bases of some mountain ranges, and other habitat areas. Tell the children to draw in the physical habitat features that fit with the plant pictures on their pages.

Next have the children cut out their pictures and paste them onto their desert scenes. (They can cut out the whole square or cut just around the outline of the plant or animal.) Then have them draw lines to connect the pictures of the plants and animals that depend on each other in some way. For example, the coyote feeds on rats, rabbits and hares, saguaro fruit, mesquite beans, and other food. So the kids should draw a line from the coyote to the jackrabbit, the pack rat, the saguaro, and the mesquite.

When everyone is done, discuss the interrelationships the children have discovered. (Use the information provided here to help with the discussion.) Also talk about how important the non-living parts of the environment (soil, water, sunlight) are to all the living things. Discuss what might happen if some parts of the community disappeared. For example, what would happen to the saguaro cactus community if all the saguaros eventually died off? (Many of the other desert plants that depend on the saguaro for shade and many of the animals that depend on it for food, water, or shade could eventually die.)

BRANCHING OUT

- Teach the children the words *herbivore* (an animal that eats plants), *carnivore* (an animal that eats other animals), and *scavenger* (an animal that eats dead animal or plant material). Then have them find the carnivores, herbivores, and scavengers on the two picture pages.

- Have the kids research the Mojave Desert, the Chihuahuan Desert, or the Great Basin Desert and draw a scene showing the plants, animals, and landforms that might be found there. Then have them compare the communities they just drew to their Sonoran Desert scenes. How are both desert communities alike? How are they different?

INFORMATION ABOUT THE PICTURE PAGES

- **Coyote:** Feeds at night on mice and other rodents, rabbits and hares, and sometimes mule deer and pronghorn antelope. Also eats saguaro cactus fruit, mesquite beans, and other plant parts. Sometimes digs burrows, which it goes into to escape heat.

- **Ringtail:** Related to a raccoon. Eats birds, insects, kangaroo rats, pack rats, and lizards. Also eats cactus fruit. Usually lives on rock ledges or near water. Is eaten by bobcats, great horned owls, and other large predators.

- **Desert Grasses:** Grow in many parts of the Sonoran Desert. Provide food for mule deer, rodents, and other herbivores.

- **Desert Tortoise:** Burrows in the ground to escape heat. Young often eaten by foxes, coyotes, and other predators. Feeds on desert grasses, wildflowers, and cactus fruit.
- **Prickly Pear Cactus:** Quail, doves, woodpeckers, kangaroo rats, pack rats, jackrabbits, peccaries, deer, and many other animals feed on its fruit, seeds, and stem. Many animals take shelter in its shade.

Leonard Lee Rue III   roadrunner

- **Roadrunner:** Eats lizards, snakes (even rattlesnakes), insects, and scorpions. Runs to chase prey and escape predators. Builds a nest of twigs in cholla, paloverde, or some other desert plant.
- **Saguaro Cactus:** Found on dry, rocky slopes and flats. White-winged doves and woodpeckers eat its seeds. Many animals eat its fruit. Many animals also nest in the trunk, including elf owls, Gila woodpeckers, and cactus wrens.
- **Peccary:** Small piglike animal that lives in thickets and travels in small bands. Feeds on prickly pear cactus and acorns, as well as insects, rattlesnakes, and lizards.
- **Kangaroo Rat:** Burrows or builds mounds. Eats seeds of prickly pear, mesquite, and other plants. Also eats some insects. Provides food for owls, coyotes, snakes, and other predators. Often jumps to escape from predators.

- **Turkey Vulture:** Often nests in canyon areas. Feeds on dead animals. Important scavenger in the desert. Finds food by smell and sight.
- **Mesquite:** A spiny shrub with yellow flowers and lacy leaves. Forms tough pods that are filled with seeds. Jackrabbits, quail, kangaroo rats, ringtails, and other animals eat the seeds. Many birds nest in its branches. Provides shade for mammals and reptiles.
- **Jackrabbit:** Feeds on a variety of plants, including grasses and flowering herbs. Also eats cactus. Eaten by coyotes, bobcats, owls, and other desert predators. Large ears (one third as long as its body) help get rid of excess body heat.
- **Lubber Grasshopper:** Eats desert grasses and other vegetation. Provides food for many desert animals, including kangaroo rats, tarantulas, and elf owls.
- **Scorpion:** Hunts at night for spiders, crickets, small lizards, and other small creatures. Is eaten by roadrunners, snakes, and owls. Often hides under rocks and near plants. Female often carries young on her back until their first molt.
- **Spadefoot Toad:** Eats insects. Eaten by snakes and larger toads. Special "spades" on hind feet help it dig into ground. (See background information on page 27 for more about spadefoot toads.)
- **Sidewinder Rattlesnake:** Lives in low desert areas. Feeds on small rodents and lizards. Sometimes eaten by larger snakes, birds of prey, and roadrunners. Has a special way of moving through sand (see page 28).
- **Fringe-toed Lizard:** Found in sandy areas. Often lives in abandoned kangaroo rat burrows. Feeds on insects, flowers, and leaves. Is eaten by sidewinders, kit foxes, and birds of prey. Specially adapted for diving under sand to escape predators.
- **Mule Deer:** Is mainly a browser. Feeds on trees and shrubs, as well as grasses and other vegetation. Preyed upon by mountain lions, coyotes, bobcats, and wolves. Often travels in small herds.

Roadrunner

Fringe-toed Lizard

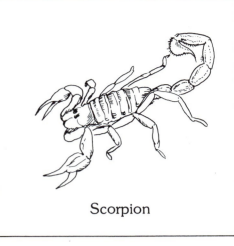

Scorpion

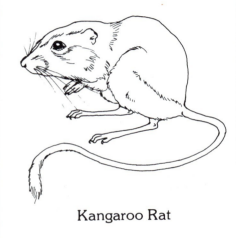

Kangaroo Rat

Jackrabbit

Spadefoot Toad

Desert Grasses

Prickly Pear Cactus

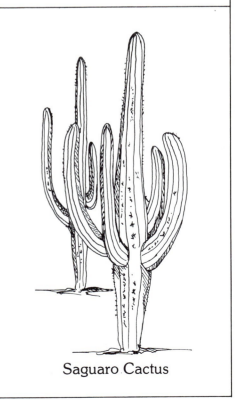

Saguaro Cactus

COPYCAT PAGE

DESERT PICTURE PAGES

Turkey Vulture

Ringtail

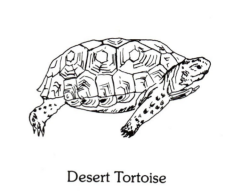

Desert Tortoise

Peccary

Lubber Grasshopper

Sidewinder

Coyote

Mesquite

Mule Deer

PEOPLE AND DESERTS

Row upon row of lush, bushy orange trees stretch across the valley and far into the distance. Beyond the orange trees lies a sprawling cotton field and beyond that, a pasture full of grazing cattle. The cattle munch hungrily on rich grasses.

You might expect to see dozens of scenes like this in the moist, green farm country of the southeastern United States. But crops and cattle are also part of another, far less likely landscape: the desert. Modern farm practices and irrigation systems have allowed people to turn acres and acres of desert into huge, unbelievably productive gardens. And uncultivated desert areas are often used as grazing grounds for cattle and sheep.

Deserts have a lot to offer—agriculturally and otherwise—and people have learned to use desert land in many ways. But if deserts aren't used carefully, some major problems can result. In this chapter we'll take a look at some of the ways people have "made the most" of deserts. We'll also look at some of the problems that human activity in deserts has caused.

A DRY EXISTENCE

To the Bushmen of Africa's Kalahari Desert, the Aborigines of the western Australian desert, and the Tuareg of the Sahara, the desert is a way of life. These and many other desert peoples have managed to survive for generations in their dry desert worlds—but they do not all make their livings in exactly the same way.

A lot of desert people get the most out of severe desert conditions by traveling from place to place. For example, the Bushmen and Aborigines are nomadic people who survive by hunting desert animals, gathering desert roots, fruits, nuts, and other food, and then moving on to richer areas when food or water supplies get low. The Tuareg are nomadic too—but they're mostly herders and traders rather than hunters and gatherers. Sheep, goats, and other livestock are their main sources of food, and they travel with their herds from one grazing ground to the next.

Some non-nomadic desert dwellers lead an agricultural life. Many of these desert farmers have managed to grow all kinds of crops in the parched landscape. In the past, for example, some Hopi Indians and other Native Americans grew special strains of corn, squash, beans, and other plants that thrived in dry desert soil. A few people are still growing these crops, and some researchers are now looking into the possibility that the drought-resistant qualities of these plants could benefit large-scale agriculture. (For more about the desert lifestyles of some Native Americans and other desert peoples, see "Desert Culture Day" on page 50.)

As the modern world closes in, the traditional lives of desert peoples are changing fast. But some of them still live by the old ways, following the customs and practices that have been a part of their cultures for ages.

DOWN ON THE FARM

Despite the desert's dryness, huge commercial farms are "cropping up" all over desert regions. The main reason for this is that technology has made water much more available for irrigation. For example, many crops—cotton, wheat, and barley, to name a few—are planted in desert areas and irrigated. But although irrigation can make deserts agriculturally productive, it has some negative side effects that can cause arid lands to become permanently *un*productive.

One of these irrigation side effects is the build-up of salt in the desert soil. The salt is left behind when irrigation water evaporates. (All water, even fresh water, contains some salt.) In some places salt can eventually accumulate to levels that make it impossible for crops and other plants to grow in the soil. This salt build-up is called *salinization*.

Another irrigation problem has to do with the use of *groundwater*. Groundwater is water that lies beneath the earth's surface. Powerful pumps can suck huge amounts of this water up to irrigation systems above ground, and the crops get all the water they need. (Groundwater under deserts also provides drinking water for thousands of people who live in deserts, and it's often used in desert mining operations.) Normally, groundwater supplies are replenished by rainwater and by other water on the earth's surface that trickles down through the soil. But in a lot of dry areas, groundwater supplies are being depleted because they can't replenish themselves fast enough to keep up with growing demands. Groundwater being pumped in some deserts was actually laid down thousands or even millions of years ago, when the climate was much wetter. In many places, this "fossil water" is literally being used up.

A DESTRUCTIVE PATTERN

One of the biggest consequences of depleting groundwater supplies is the fact that the scarcer groundwater becomes, the more expensive it is to suck it out of the ground. And when it gets too expensive to irrigate crops, the cropland is often abandoned. The fields soon dry up, and before natural vegetation can move back in and hold the soil down, the wind blows much of the soil away. Whatever rain that falls can also cause erosion. (Rain in the desert is rare, but when it does fall it's often torrential. Desert downpours can carry away a lot of soil.) Before too long the eroded area is unfit for most plant and animal life.

LIFELESS LANDS IN THE MAKING

Salinization and the overuse of groundwater reserves are just two examples of the ways *desertification* can occur. Desertification is the transformation of an area of land from one that supports life to one that can support far less life—or no life at all. Since arid and semi-arid places are so fragile ecologically, they are particularly vulnerable to the process of desertification.

One of the main causes of desertification—and maybe *the* main cause in the United States—is erosion brought about by overgrazing. Many desert and semi-desert areas in the West have provided some ranchers with inexpensive rangeland for their cattle or sheep. But livestock can munch a lot of vegetation, and when too many of them feed in one place, they can easily strip the land of most of its cover. Left exposed, the desert soil erodes away, just as it does on abandoned agricultural fields. And the overgrazed area loses its usefulness to people, to livestock, and to most of the wildlife that once lived there.

All kinds of other human activities can lead to desertification too. In North American deserts, for example, a recreational pastime is causing big trouble. This pastime—driving motorcycles, minibikes, Jeeps, and other off-road vehicles (ORVs) in the desert—has become very popular. But ORVs tear up desert plants and soil and destroy wildlife habitat. And although some desert areas are legally off-limits to ORV users, the signs separating these areas from ORV "play" areas are often ignored.

In some arid parts of Africa, fuelwood collection has become a big part of the desertification problem. Many of the people who live in these areas can't afford to buy oil, gas, and other fuels for heating their homes and for cooking. So they cut down trees and shrubs for fuel, leaving the land stripped of its cover. In some areas the stripped land has become severely eroded, and overgrazing and overcultivation have added to the problem. As a result, crop and livestock production hasn't kept pace with human population growth—and millions of people have suffered.

LANDS OF PLENTY

It seems contradictory to classify deserts as rich, productive lands. But when you think about it, that's just what they are. Not only are they rich in plant and animal life, they are also rich in resources that people use. For example, much of the petroleum that keeps our cars and industry running is drawn from reserves underneath deserts, and a lot of deserts are mined for copper, diamonds, phosphate, silver, uranium, and other minerals. Mineral-rich desert soil and the almost never-ending "supply" of sunshine can produce lush fields of cotton, wheat, and other crops if people provide the water. And some arid areas can make relatively cheap rangeland.

In many places, though, these desert resources are being overused, and the result is desertification. Each year, an estimated 15 million acres are lost to desertification, and some scientists feel that this loss could eventually affect the earth's atmosphere and the world's ecology. To help avoid or slow desertification, resource managers are trying to regulate the amount of water used, the number of cattle grazed, and other activities that threaten desert areas. And some scientists are looking into possible ways that ravaged deserts might be restored to their normal, "healthy" state. But the pressures on arid lands are growing, and most researchers agree that it will take a lot of time, dedication, and money to stop the desertification trend.

Lost in the Desert

Listen to a desert story and talk about safety in the desert and elsewhere.

Objectives:
Name four things you should do if you get lost outside. Talk about ways to prepare for a hike in the desert.

Ages:
Primary and Intermediate

Materials:
- *"Read-to-me" story on pages 48 and 49*
- *chalkboard or easel paper*

Subject:
Safety

 n this activity you can use a desert story to talk about what to do if you're lost—not only in the desert, but anywhere.

Start by telling the kids to listen carefully as you read "First Day in the Desert," below. After you finish reading, divide the group into smaller groups of four or five. Tell each group to think back over the story and identify the mistakes they think Jason made that led to his bad situation. Then, using the list of mistakes following the story, start a safety discussion by asking one of the groups to name one of the things Jason shouldn't have done. (You might want to have the groups write down the mistakes they think Jason made before you begin your discussion.) After discussing one mistake, go on to another group and ask them to name something else Jason shouldn't have done. Keep going from group to group until you've talked about all the mistakes they caught, then discuss any of the ones they didn't catch.

Afterward, ask the kids what Jason did that probably kept his situation from becoming even worse. (He found a shelter out of the sun.) Explain that it's important to find shelter whenever you're lost outside—especially if you're lost in the desert. And in hot places like deserts, it's important to be as inactive as possible during the heat of the day to keep from overheating.

Tell the kids that Jason eventually did something else that helped him. After he sprained his ankle he stopped moving around and stayed in one place. Staying put—whether you're injured or not—makes it easier for people to find you.

Next ask the kids to think about what Jason could have done if his parents hadn't found him when they did. Explain that, if possible, you should somehow signal for help if you're lost. For example, if Jason had thought about safety, he might have carried a small mirror with him so he could signal with it by "flashing" it in the sun. Or he could have carried a whistle with him. Ask the kids if they can think of any other ways Jason could have signaled for help. (Explain that, in the desert, continuously yelling for help isn't a good idea. Experienced desert travelers recommend that a person lost in the desert keep his or her mouth closed as much as possible to slow down dehydration.)

To reinforce your discussion, write the following safety rules on the board or a large piece of paper:
- Stay calm
- Seek shelter
- Stay put
- Signal

(For another safety story, see "Lost," *Ranger Rick,* August 1984, pages 9-11.)

FIRST DAY IN THE DESERT

Jason jumped out of bed as soon as the sun started to rise. This was going to be his first full day at his new home in the desert, and he was way too excited to sleep any later. *The desert!* he thought. *I actually live in the desert now!* It was a whole different world from the New England town where his family had lived till now.

Jason had been reading about roadrunners, kangaroo rats, Gila monsters, and other desert animals, and he couldn't wait to see some for himself. In a flash he put on his shorts and gym shoes. *It's too warm for a shirt,* he thought.

Jason's sister and parents were still asleep, so he tiptoed down the stairs and toward the back door. He stepped out into the sunshine and looked around. In the distance a mountain range rose up from the desert floor. It didn't look too far away, and he decided he could probably get there and back before breakfast. He started walking at a steady pace.

There was a lot to look at along the way. Jason went down one hill and up another, looking at strange new plants and colorful rocks. Once he came across some snake tracks along a dry creek bed and followed them up into a stand of mesquite. He couldn't find the snake itself, so after a while he gave up his search.

Jason scrambled out of the brush a couple of minutes later. But when he looked in the direction he thought the mountains should have been, they weren't there. Instead, they were behind him. "Wow—I sure got turned around in those trees," he said as he started off once again.

Soon Jason noticed that the desert was really starting to heat up—*fast*. He began to feel hot and thirsty. And the mountains didn't look like they were any closer than when he'd started out. "Maybe I should just go home," he muttered, suddenly realizing that he wasn't only hot and thirsty, but hungry too.

Jason turned around slowly and started hiking home. But after a while he began to get worried. Nothing looked very familiar. His heart began to pound as he realized he was lost.

Squinting up toward the sky, Jason noticed that the sun was getting higher and more intense. Suddenly all Jason could think about was how much he wanted to be home with his family, drinking a nice cold glass of water. In all his life, Jason had never felt so thirsty. He started walking fast, wondering frantically how long a person can go without water before dying.

There was a hill up ahead. Jason broke into a run and raced to the top of it. He looked around in *every* direction. No houses anywhere—just miles and miles of hot desert. Jason could feel tears forming and he rubbed his eyes. "I've *got* to get home," he sobbed.

Way off to one side there was a patch of bushes. Jason took off running down the slope toward them, hoping his house would turn up on the other side. But tears blurred his vision and he didn't see the small rock that jutted out near the base of the hill. He hit the rock hard with the side of his foot and fell, twisting his ankle. A sharp, shooting pain raced up his leg when he tried to stand up. There was no way he could travel any farther.

Jason sank back down to the ground, feeling helpless and miserable. He forced himself to think about what he should do and decided that, for now, the best thing would be to get out of the sun. A clump of mesquite lay off to his right, and Jason slowly made his way over to it on his hands and knees. Crawling into the shade, he decided that he really needed to rest for awhile. As he rested he began to calm down. He thought about the day so far and realized some of the mistakes he'd made.

Suddenly Jason heard a faint, muffled sound that made his heart leap. He held his breath, straining to hear it again.

"Jason! Can you hear us?" It was Jason's dad.

"Dad! I'm over here!" Jason yelled as loud as he possibly could.

His mother answered him. "Stay where you are. We'll be there in a minute!"

Jason sighed and closed his eyes. *Looks as if life in the desert is going to be exciting,* he thought. Already he'd learned a lot—the hard way—about his new desert home.

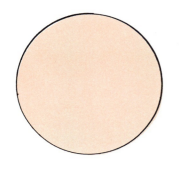

JASON'S MISTAKES

(We've listed them in the order they occurred.)

1. **He didn't wear the right kind of clothing for a walk in the desert.** It's tempting to dress as lightly as possible for a hike in the hot desert sun. That's why Jason wore only shorts and gym shoes. But the desert sun is strong, and a bad sunburn can happen before you know it. Long pants, a long-sleeved shirt, and a hat offer good protection.

Being "well-dressed" in the desert can also help prevent dehydration by trapping sweat against your skin. This layer of sweat evaporates more slowly than it would if you weren't wearing enough clothes, and the slower rate of evaporation can keep your body cooler longer.

2. **He went out alone without telling anyone where he was going.** If you're in an unfamiliar area, it's never a good idea to go exploring by yourself. *(continued next page)*

And it's also not a good idea to go somewhere without letting somebody know where you're going. In Jason's case, the least he could have done was to leave a note telling which direction he was headed.

3. **He didn't take any water.** No desert hiker should be without water—even if the hike's a short one. A good guideline is one gallon (3.8 l) of water per person per day.

4. **He didn't pay close enough attention to where he was going.** Jason wandered here and there, and then got mixed up when he followed snake tracks into a stand of mesquite. He would've been less likely to get lost if he'd walked in more of a straight line.

5. **He panicked when he realized he was lost.** When you panic it's hard to think clearly and you're more likely to use bad judgement. In Jason's case, panic led to a sprained ankle.

Desert Culture Day

Give a presentation and create an exhibit on a people who live in the desert.

Objective:
Describe the lifestyle of one group of desert people.

Ages:
Intermediate and Advanced

Materials:
- *small slips of paper*
- *desert research books*
- *copies of page 56*
- *materials for making exhibits (crayons, markers, drawing paper, cardboard, and so on)*

Subject:
Social Studies

Nomadic traders, hunter-gatherers, and farmers all have found ways to live in the harsh environment of the desert. In fact, some cultures have survived in the desert for more than 30,000 years. Try this activity to help your kids learn about some different desert peoples and their ways of life.

First write the words *Aborigines, Bushmen, Hopi Indians,* and *Tuareg* on separate slips of paper and put them in a bag. (Each term is the name of a particular group of desert people. The Hopi Indians are just one example of Native American desert dwellers. If you have a large group you might want to include other arid land Native Americans, such as the Apache, Navajo, Papago, Pima, Yuma, Zuni, and others.) Next divide the kids into four groups and have each group pick a slip from the bag. Tell the kids that they'll be participating in a Desert Culture Day.

On Desert Culture Day each group will give a presentation on the people they picked. They'll also display an exhibit that they've created to go along with their presentation. The groups will need to research basic information about their desert people, such as where the people live, what they eat, how they dress, what kind of dwellings they live in, how religion affects their lives, and so on. (See the list at the end of the activity for information about each group of desert people. If you're working with younger kids, you might want to give them copies of the information to help them with their research.)

Explain to the kids that they should focus on traditional lifestyles. As with most native cultures, those of many desert peoples are being lost as modern society "moves in." But some members of these cultures still practice traditional ways of life. Some of the groups may want to include in their presentations a short discussion of how modern society has affected the desert people they picked.

To give the kids some ideas for exhibits they can create, suggest these possibilities:

- shadowbox scene (camel caravan, village, hunting party, and so on)
- model of a typical house or shelter
- life-sized models of tools or hunting weapons
- drawings of how they dress
- maps showing where they live
- posters showing what they wear for special ceremonies
- samples of the kinds of foods they grow or gather

To split up the work, have each child research one aspect of the desert people's lives. Then the groups can create one exhibit or several small exhibits, based on each group member's research. For example, in the Hopi group two children might work together to research traditional Hopi dwellings and then make a model. Another child might research and then draw pictures of traditional Hopi dress, and another might concentrate on traditional Hopi foods and the ways these Native Americans managed to grow what they needed in the dry soil before modern equipment became available.

On Desert Culture Day have the kids set up their exhibits around the room. Then have each group give a short presentation about their desert people. Each child might want to say a sentence or two about what he or she researched. Then let everyone walk around and look at the other groups' exhibits.

The kids can also sample some desert fare. For example, you can discuss oasis-loving trees such as date palms as the kids munch on dates. You might also get the kids to try a little goat's milk (available at health food stores) while you talk about nomadic tribes and their herds of goats,

camels, and cattle. Or you can pop a batch of popcorn and talk about how important corn was to the Native Americans who farmed the desert soils of the Southwest.

Below is a brief look at the traditional lifestyles of four different desert groups. (You might want to remind the kids that, even though we've used the present tense, the information we've given represents traditional lifestyles that are no longer as prominent as they once were.) *Note:* To reinforce what the children have learned about these groups, pass out copies of the Desert Culture Match-Up on page 56.

Aborigines of the Australian Deserts
- Nomadic hunter-gatherers.
- Women gather turtles, yams, berries, nuts, roots, leaves, honey, and insects.
- Men hunt emus, kangaroos, lizards, geese, and other game.
- Get water from water holes. Follow the rains so they can drink from the pools the rains make.
- Sometimes make shelters (windbreaks) out of grass or leafy branches but usually just make depressions in the ground.
- Usually wear no clothing but occasionally wear animal skins.
- Hunt with spears and boomerangs. Also use the dingo (a type of wild dog) to help track and run down kangaroos.

Bushmen of the Kalahari Desert in Africa
- Nomadic hunter-gatherers.
- Women gather melons, bulbs, roots, tubers, nuts, fruits, and leafy vegetables.
- Men hunt giraffes, wildebeest, antelope, and other game.
- Get water from melons, roots, tubers, depressions in logs, and the stomach contents of animals that they kill. Sometimes store water in ostrich eggshells, which they bury in the ground for use during drought.
- Construct shelters using branches covered with grass.
- Wear pieces of leather or no clothing.
- Hunt with spears and also with bows and poison-tipped arrows. Use digging sticks to dig up roots and tubers.
- Camp in one place as long as the area will sustain them, and then move on to another area. Often plan their moves so that they arrive just when wild plants are ready for harvesting.

Hopi Indians of the Southwestern United States
- Farmers. Grow corn, beans, squash, and cotton.
- Women make and decorate pottery, dye yarn, grind corn, and make meals.
- Men tend the fields, weave, and hunt rabbits, deer, antelope, and other game.
- Construct large, several-storied homes of adobe and rock.
- Men wear cotton breechcloths and cotton kilts. On ceremonial occasions, women wear cotton cloth wrapped around their bodies with the left shoulder bare. (After the arrival of the Spanish, the Hopis started tending sheep and weaving wool as well.)
- Hunt with throwing sticks, bows and arrows, and clubs. They also set traps and raise turkeys.

Tuareg of the Sahara Desert in Africa
- Nomadic traders and herdsmen. Move about in areas where rainfall provides pasture for their camels, goats, and sheep. Trade salt.
- Women milk livestock and prepare meals.
- Men tend the herds.
- Milk is the main food item along with meat from their herd animals. They get tea, grain, and dates from merchants at oases.
- Make tents of goatskin or sometimes mats woven from palm leaves.
- Men and women wear loosely fitting garments. Men wear a veil that they wrap around their heads and across their faces.

The Spreading Desert

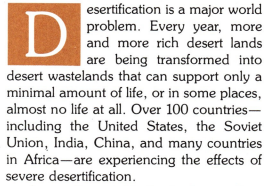

Desertification is a major world problem. Every year, more and more rich desert lands are being transformed into desert wastelands that can support only a minimal amount of life, or in some places, almost no life at all. Over 100 countries—including the United States, the Soviet Union, India, China, and many countries in Africa—are experiencing the effects of severe desertification.

As we discussed in the background information on pages 46 and 47, there are many causes of desertification. In this activity, your group can learn what desertification is and some of the reasons it is a growing problem around the world.

First give each person a copy of page 57, a large piece of easel paper or construction paper, and glue or tape. Have the children cut out the squares and spread them out. Then lead a group discussion about the reasons that deserts around the world are in trouble. As you discuss the problems, have them make desertification charts. Here's how:

First have each person write the word *desert* in big letters on the left-hand side of his or her paper, and draw a box around it. Explain that this box represents a healthy desert area in the United States, with rich soils and a variety of plant and animal life. It also has large supplies of water beneath the ground. (Explain that water found beneath the earth's surface is called *groundwater.*) Now have the children look at the squares they cut out

and find the ones that represent a way desert lands are being used. (mining, grazing cattle and sheep, cities and towns, off-road vehicles, crops, industries, park and recreation areas) Have them paste these uses, one below the other, to the right of the box labeled *desert*. Then have them draw lines from the desert to each type of land use.

Next have the kids search for the cards that show how these land uses help people. They should paste each one of these next to the appropriate land use so that the two are connected (see illustration).

Now have the kids paste the four bigger blocks (can deplete groundwater supplies, causes a lot of salt to build up in the soil, causes soil erosion, and causes native plants to be destroyed) to the right of the ways desert land uses help people. Then have the kids draw lines from the land use benefits to the harmful effects the land use has on the desert. (Have them use a different color for each use.) Here are some of the ways they can connect the boxes:

- Sheep and cattle that are allowed to overgraze can destroy native plants and cause soil erosion.
- Crop irrigation can cause salt to build up in the soil and can deplete groundwater supplies.
- Mining uses a lot of water and can deplete groundwater supplies. It also destroys native plants that once lived where the mining is taking place.
- Industry often uses groundwater supplies.
- Cities use groundwater, and construction in and around cities often destroys plants and habitats.
- Off-road vehicles disrupt soil and destroy native plants and habitats.
- Parks can become overused and hikers can trample plants and cause soil erosion.

After the children have connected the land uses and benefits with the problems they can cause, discuss each one. Then have them write *desert wasteland* at the far right of their papers, and draw a box around these words. Tell them to finish the

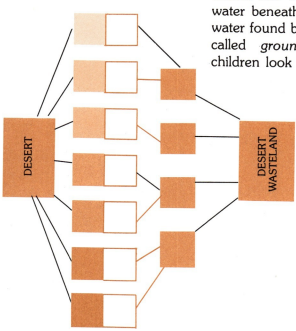

chart by drawing lines from the four problems to this final square. Explain that desertification transforms varied desert lands into desert wastelands. Point out that nobody is intentionally out to destroy the desert. It's just that people need to make a living or a profit, want to live where they choose, and often use the land to meet their needs without thinking about the consequences of their actions. Many people also don't realize how fragile desert lands are. And when land is destroyed by overuse, less of it is available for use by future generations.

Ask the children if they can think of some solutions to the problems on their chart. (With such a complicated problem as desertification, the children cannot know all the consequences of various land uses or understand how to really solve the problems. But it's important that they realize that solutions to environmental problems often mean personal sacrifices on everybody's part.) Here are some questions you can ask the kids to get them thinking about solutions:

- Would you be willing to stop riding your bike in a favorite area if you knew it caused erosion and hurt the plants that grow there? (Tie this in with off-road vehicle use.)

- Would you be willing to have less variety at the grocery store (not as many kinds of foods to pick from) if it meant helping to protect land in desert areas? (Tie this in with the fact that many of our foods grow in the desert, including many off-season fruits and vegetables. In all, about 20% of the nation's total agricultural output depends on desert lands.)
- Would you be willing to use less water every day if it would help groundwater supplies replenish themselves?
- Would you be willing to give up your allowance to pay for water-saving irrigation equipment? (Explain that many of the solutions to desertification cost a lot of money. But if desertification is allowed to continue, the costs people will be forced to pay in the future will be much higher.)

Then discuss some of the solutions scientists are currently working on, such as:

- transporting water from far away—even hauling icebergs from Antarctica (This would be very expensive and use a lot of energy.)
- finding a cheap way to desalinize (remove the salt from) seawater
- developing new crops that can grow in very dry areas without needing to be irrigated
- developing new crops that can grow in very salty soil
- monitoring cattle and sheep on desert lands to prevent overgrazing
- finding ways to reclaim desert wasteland and "bring it back to life"
- finding ways to make irrigation more efficient so that it doesn't use as much water

BRANCHING OUT

To show children how a salt build-up in the soil can affect plants, have them plant two sets of bean seeds in two separate flats (each about 8 × 12″ [20 × 30 cm]). In one of the flats, have them mix two cups of salt with the soil.

Every few days, water both flats with fresh water. Also sprinkle more salt on the surface of the flat that has salt mixed with the soil. Compare what happens in the flats over the next week or so. (The seeds in the salty flat should not germinate because of the salt. Too much salt in the soil can draw water out of a seed and prevent it from germinating. If the "control" flat seeds also did not germinate, there is probably something wrong with the seeds and you should try it again with new seeds.)

Desert Quest

Find the answers to desert-related questions and compete in a desert contest.

Objectives:
Research the answers to desert-related questions.
Discuss three unusual desert-related facts.

Ages:
Advanced

Materials:
- **paper and pencils**
- **reference books**

Subject:
Science

Holding a desert research contest is a great way to help your kids learn some fascinating desert facts. To get started, pass out copies of the questions listed at the end of the activity. (The answers are listed on the inside back cover.) Then divide the group into five or six teams. Tell the kids that they'll have a certain amount of time to answer as many of the questions as they can. For example, the deadline for answering questions might be two weeks from the day the contest begins. To find their answers, the kids will have to do some research—and for some questions they may have to "dig" for the information they need. That could mean looking up information not only in encyclopedias, but also in other reference books and maybe even periodicals. (You can either give the kids some research time every day or so or let them work completely on their own time.)

Each team member can work on all of the questions, or else each person can be responsible for answering only one or two of the questions. (You might want to leave it up to each team to decide how to divide the workload.) Tell the kids that they don't have to find answers to all of the questions. But they won't receive points for unanswered questions or for questions answered incorrectly.

Have the kids write down the sources of their answers. (Even if they think they know an answer without having to look it up, they should try to find a source that backs up the answer.) Explain that, whenever they research something, it's important to keep records of their sources of information. That way they can easily find the information again if they need to refer back to it.

On the day of the deadline, have all of the teams neatly write their answers and reference sources on a piece of paper and hand them in. Then check their answers against the answers we provide. Score a point for each correct answer and 0 points for each unanswered question or wrong answer. (Keep in mind that some of the kids' answers may be a little different from ours for a couple of reasons. First, the kids may have to rely on older sources of information that have become outdated by newer research and findings. Second, some of our answers—especially those involving numbers—are approximate, since exact answers aren't known and vary slightly from one source to the next. As long as the kids did their research they should probably get credit for an answer, even if it's different from ours.)

When you're finished checking the answers, go through all the questions with the kids. Then reveal the winning team!

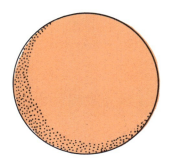

DESERT QUEST QUESTIONS

1. What makes the skin of some Tuareg nomads turn blue?
2. Name four ways some desert people use camels.
3. What percentage of the earth's surface is desert?
4. What are gibbers and where are they found?
5. What important liquid energy source is found under many desert areas?
6. Many scientists think that certain kinds of desert plants are among the oldest living things in the world. Name one of these plants.
7. About how tall can a saguaro (sah-WAH-ro) cactus get to be?
8. What is a tagilmust?
9. What do Bushmen store in ostrich eggshells?
10. Why is oil sprayed on sand dunes in some deserts?
11. What well-known ancient culture thrived in a huge African oasis?
12. Where does a lot of water that irrigates California's Imperial Valley come from?
13. What continent has the largest desert and what is the desert's name?
14. What is a seif and what does the word *seif* mean?
15. The fruit of what cactus is a favorite of the Papago Indians?
16. What animal sometimes helps Australian Aborigines when they go hunting?
17. On which continent do scientists think the first camel evolved?
18. What valley represents the world's largest oasis?
19. Which desert-dwelling Native Americans are now known as the "ancient ones"?
20. Which large, stony desert did Genghis Khan and his troops ride through on their way to conquering China?
21. About how much water per person per day should you take with you on a trip into the desert?
22. What does the Mongolian word *gobi* mean?
23. How did the Joshua tree get its name?
24. What desert insects become very destructive when they gather in groups to swarm?
25. How can the oil of the desert plant called jojoba (ho-HO-ba) benefit the sperm whale?
26. Why do certain beetles in the Namib Desert often stand at the crest of a dune with their abdomens pointing up into the air?
27. What do the desert birds known as sandgrouse have in common with a sponge?
28. What is Pueblo Bonito and where is it located?
29. What substance do camels frequently carry to market in blocks?
30. What's a kuipad?

COPYCAT PAGE   DESERT CULTURE MATCH-UP

Match each picture on the right with one of the people on the left by writing the letters in the blanks.

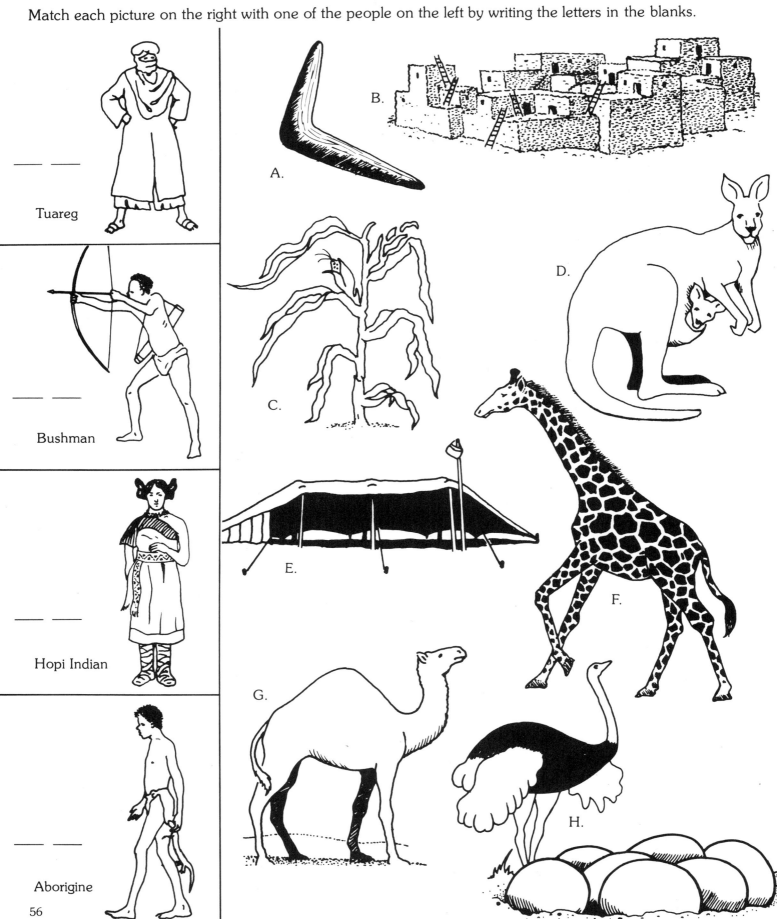

___ ___ ___

Tuareg

___ ___ ___

Bushman

___ ___ ___

Hopi Indian

___ ___ ___

Aborigine

56

A.

B.

C.

D.

E.

F.

G.

H.

setting aside land for parks

provides recreation

can deplete groundwater supplies

allowing large numbers of sheep and cattle to graze

provides beef, mutton, leather, and wool for people

causes a lot of salt to build up in the soil

growing crops using irrigation

provides all kinds of crops (such as wheat and cotton)

allowing off-road vehicle use

provides recreation

causes soil erosion

mining for minerals and drilling for oil

provides oil and minerals for people to use

building towns and cities

provides a place for people to live

causes native plants to be destroyed

setting up industries

provides jobs for people

CRAFTY CORNER

Here are some desert art and craft ideas you can use to complement many of the activities in the first five sections.

Earth Paintings

Make paint from soil and use it to create a desert scene or symbol.

Ages:
Primary, Intermediate, and Advanced

Materials:
- *shovel or hand spade*
- *soil or sand*
- *small cups (one or several per person)*
- *white glue*
- *water*
- *paintbrushes*
- *thin cardboard*
- *paper towels*
- *pencils*
- *pictures of Native American pottery, weavings, and other crafts (optional)*

Subjects:
Art and Crafts

Like most crafts, those of the ancient Native American desert dwellers incorporate many different symbols and designs. For example, some pottery was decorated with religious symbols or pictures of animals that were important to the Indians. The designs were often painted onto the pottery. The "paints" themselves were made from plants and other natural materials.

Your kids can make their own "earth paint" out of soil or sand and then use the paint to create a design or symbol of something that's important in their lives. First give each person a small cup and take the group outside. Dig into the ground a little and break up some of the soil, pulling out rocks and other debris. Then have the kids collect some soil in their cups. A half-full cup of soil should be enough for a couple of paintings. (You might want to give the

kids two or three cups each so they can collect soils of different colors. If you want, you can also have them collect sand.)

Have the kids crumble their samples into a powdery consistency. Then have them combine two parts soil (or a mixture of soil and sand) with two parts water and one part white glue. They should stir these ingredients into a soupy mixture.

Next pass out a piece of thin white cardboard to each person and tell the kids to think up a design or symbol that represents something that's important in their lives. (You might want to show the kids pictures of southwestern Indian pottery, weavings, and other crafts to give them some ideas.) Or they can think up a desert scene to paint. Have the kids sketch the symbol or scene onto the cardboard, then have them paint in their sketches with their "earth paint." (When the paintings are dry, the soil will be fixed to the cardboard and won't smudge off.) Afterward, have them talk about their paintings to the rest of the group, explaining what their particular symbols mean.

To clean up the paintbrushes, just soak them in warm water until the soil and glue come off. Then wipe them dry with paper towels.

Make A Giant Saguaro Cactus

Using paper-mache and chicken wire, make a life-sized saguaro cactus.

Ages:
Intermediate and Advanced

(continued next page)

Building a life-sized saguaro cactus can be an exciting group project and the finished saguaro can be used in all kinds of desert-related activities. Here's how to do it:

1. Getting Started
- Find a large workspace. Outside is best, but you can build this huge

cactus in a corner of the room. Be sure to protect the floor by putting down a piece of plastic or cloth before you begin.
Note: On the day before you plan to work on the cactus, be sure to tell your group to bring in old clothes or painting aprons. (Paper-mache

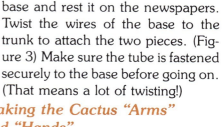

Materials:
- *pictures of saguaro cactuses*
- *chicken wire, 3' (.9 m) wide and 12' (3.6 m) long*
- *wire cutters*
- *scissors*
- *flour (5-10 pounds)*
- *lots of old newspaper*
- *washtub or large bucket*
- *4-8 small buckets*
- *warm water*
- *large mixing spoon*
- *white paper towels or napkins*
- *spray paint or poster paint*
- *round toothpicks*
- *soil or sand*
- *white glue*
- *paintbrushes*
- *small cups*
- *tape (optional)*

Subject:
Crafts

paste can get all over everything, but easily washes out of most fabrics.)

2. Making the Trunk
- Cut a 3-foot (.9-m) × 4½-foot (1.4-m) piece of chicken wire and roll it into a 4½-foot (1.4-m) long tube with a 1-foot (.3-m) diameter.
- Twist the exposed ends of the wire together to hold the edges of the tube in place. (Figure 1)

3. Making the Base
- Cut a 3-foot (.9-m) square piece of chicken wire. Then place a 5-6 pound stack of newspapers in the middle of this square piece of wire.
- Starting at one of the corners, cut a straight line through the chicken wire to the corner of the newspaper. Do the same for the other three corners. (Figure 2)
- Bend the wire sides up around the stack of newspapers and connect the sides by twisting the exposed ends of the wire.

4. Connecting the Base to the Trunk
- To attach the tube (or trunk of the cactus, from step 2) to the base, first bend all exposed wire sticking out of the tube toward the inside of the tube. Then insert the tube into the

base and rest it on the newspapers. Twist the wires of the base to the trunk to attach the two pieces. (Figure 3) Make sure the tube is fastened securely to the base before going on. (That means a lot of twisting!)

5. Making the Cactus "Arms" and "Hands"
- Cut two pieces of chicken wire, each 2 feet (.6 m) × 3 feet (.9 m). Roll each piece of chicken wire into a 3-foot (.9-m) long tube, twisting the wire ends together to hold the edges of the tube in place. (Figure 4)
- Cut a 2-foot (.6-m) section off each tube so that you have two 2-foot tubes (the "arms") and two 1-foot tubes (the "hands"). (Figure 5)

6. Attaching the Arms to the Trunk
- To insert the first arm, cut a 5-inch (12.5-cm) diameter hole into the cactus trunk about 3½ feet (1.1 m) from the floor.
- Slip one of the 2-foot (.6-m) arms all the way through the hole and attach it to the other side of the trunk by twisting the exposed wire on the arm to the trunk. Also twist the exposed wires sticking out of the cactus holes around the arm to make it more secure. (Figure 6)
- Make another 5-inch (12.5-cm) hole on the opposite side of the trunk about 2 inches (5 cm) above the first one. Attach the second arm just as you did the first. (Figure 6)

7. Attaching the Hands to the Arms
- To attach the 1-foot (.3-m) hand pieces, cut a 5-inch (12.5-cm) circle out of the top of each arm, right at the end of the 2-foot (.6-m) length. Then insert the hand sections into each circle so that they rest on the "bottom" end of the arm piece. Twist the exposed wires to secure each hand section. (Figure 7)
- Stuff paper balls made from crumpled newspaper into the top of the trunk and the top of each hand. (Figure 8)

Bruce Norfleet

(continued next page)

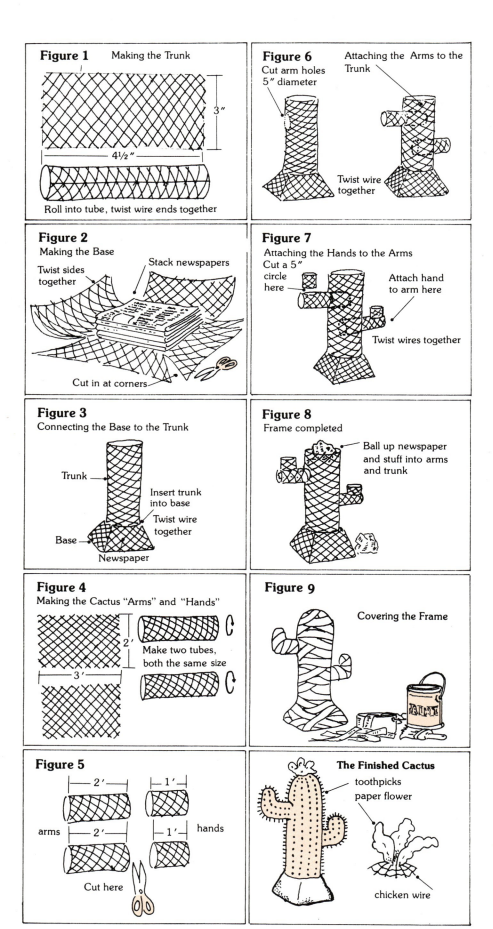

Figure 1 Making the Trunk

3″

4½″

Roll into tube, twist wire ends together

Figure 2
Making the Base

Twist sides together

Stack newspapers

Cut in at corners

Figure 3
Connecting the Base to the Trunk

Trunk

Insert trunk into base

Twist wire together

Base

Newspaper

Figure 4
Making the Cactus "Arms" and "Hands"

2′

3′

Make two tubes, both the same size

Figure 5

2′   1′

arms

2′   1′   hands

Cut here

Figure 6 Attaching the Arms to the Trunk
Cut arm holes 5″ diameter

Twist wire together

Figure 7
Attaching the Hands to the Arms
Cut a 5″ circle here

Attach hand to arm here

Twist wires together

Figure 8
Frame completed

Ball up newspaper and stuff into arms and trunk

Figure 9

Covering the Frame

The Finished Cactus

toothpicks
paper flower

chicken wire

8. Covering the Frame with Paper-Mache

- Have one group mix up the paper-mache paste by combining 5 pounds (2.3 kg) of flour with 20 cups (4.8 l) of warm water in a large bucket or washtub.
- Have another group cut newspaper into strips 6-8 inches (15-20 cm) long.
- Then have the kids work in shifts to cover the base and trunk of the cactus with paper-mache. (Pour the paste into several small buckets so the kids can spread out while they work on the cactus.)
- After the trunk and base are covered, have them work on the arms. Be careful not to use too much paper-mache: Wet newspaper is heavy and may cause the cactus's arms to droop.
- To give the base of the cactus a more natural look, cover it with white paper towels or napkins. (Apply them right on top of the wet newspaper.) Then mix up some "earth paint" and paint the base (see page 58).

9. Finishing the Cactus

- Allow the cactus to dry completely, then paint it with green spray paint or green poster paint. *Remember to use spray paint only in a well-ventilated area!*
- For a flowering saguaro, cut a small circle of chicken wire and tape it to the top of the cactus trunk. Then use paper towels or napkins to make a bunch of flowers. Slip the flowers in the chicken wire and fluff them out to look full and to cover the wire.
- As a final step, have the kids give the cactus its spines by sticking round toothpicks into the trunk, arms, and hands of the cactus in vertical rows.

APPENDIX

Questions, Questions, and More Questions

1. Name two characteristics that all deserts have in common. (high rate of evaporation, low humidity, fewer than 10 inches [25 cm] of rainfall per year)
2. True or false: All deserts are hot. (False. Some deserts are cold during the winter and get over half their moisture from snow.)
3. What is a rain shadow desert? (a desert that forms on the "dry side" of a mountain range)
4. The big ears of the jackrabbit and fennec fox are examples of _____ evolution. (convergent)
5. Plants that quickly sprout, flower, and make new seeds when it rains in the desert are called _____. (ephemerals)
6. Name two cold deserts. (See the "Deserts of the World" insert.)
7. Some insects, lizards, and snakes that live in fog deserts get drinking water when fog _____ on their bodies. (condenses)
8. The action of _____ and _____ erodes rock and causes buttes, canyons, and arches to form in many desert areas. (wind, water)
9. What's the difference between a hot desert and a cold desert? (Hot deserts have high temperatures during most of the year. Cold deserts have temperatures that often fall below freezing for at least part of the year.)
10. True or false: The tracks of vehicles and the trails of animals can remain visible in desert soils for as long as 50 years. (True)
11. Camels store _____ in their humps. (fat)
12. True or false: Thousands of years ago, the Sahara was a green, lush land of rivers and grasslands. (True)
13. True or false: On the average, desert plants have smaller leaves than non-desert plants. (True)
14. Name three ways animals escape desert heat. (by being nocturnal, burrowing, finding shade, climbing into a tree or bush, estivating)
15. True or false: Of all the desert land in the world, more than half is covered with sand. (False. Only about 15% is covered with sand.)
16. What are the two largest deserts in North America? (Chihuahuan and Great Basin)
17. What is desertification? (the transformation of an area of land from one that can support life to one that can support very little life or no life at all)
18. Name two things people do that can contribute to desertification. (allow cattle and sheep to overgraze, cut down trees and shrubs for firewood, drive ORVs, over-irrigate)
19. True or false: Desertification is a problem only in Africa. (False. Desertification is a problem in many parts of the world.)
20. Which one of the following types of animals is *not* found in any desert: fish, toads, jellyfish, or frogs? (jellyfish)
21. Describe four ways plants have adapted to living in the desert. (small leaves, very deep or very shallow roots, waxy coverings, spines, water storage, transpire at night)
22. The _____ (Bushmen or Aborigines) are nomadic people who live in the Kalahari Desert of Africa. (Bushmen)
23. What is the largest desert in the world? (Sahara)
24. Over-irrigating desert lands often causes _____ to build up in desert soils. (salt)
25. True or false: Dead animals and plants take longer to decay in deserts than in rain forests. (True)
26. Which of these states is partially covered by desert—Oregon, California, Arizona, New Mexico, or Texas? (all of them)

Glossary

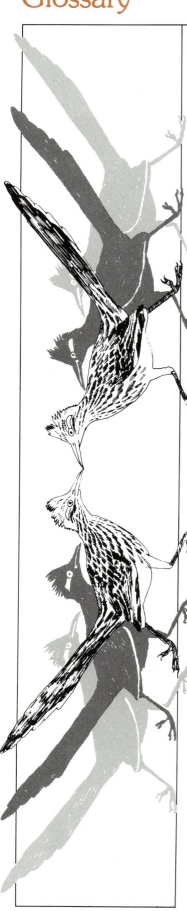

adapt—slowly evolve or change to fit the environment. For example, camels have broad feet and are adapted to walking on sand.

community—a group of plants and animals that lives in the same habitat.

convergent evolution—the process by which animals living in similar environments adapt in similar ways. For example, both the Saharan fennec fox and the North American jackrabbit have evolved big ears which release body heat.

desert—an area that receives less than 10 inches (25 cm) of rainfall a year and has a very high rate of evaporation.

desertification—the process in which land that supports life is transformed into land that can support very little life or no life at all.

drought-deciduous plants—desert plants that grow leaves during the rainy season and shed them during the dry season. The ocotillo is a drought-deciduous plant.

ecology—the study of how plants and animals interact with each other and with their environments.

estivation—a "deep sleep" that some desert animals enter. Estivation is a hot weather version of hibernation.

evaporate—to change from a liquid to a vapor.

groundwater—water that lies beneath the earth's surface.

habitat—the place where an animal lives. For example, the web-footed gecko's habitat is a sand dune.

ephemeral plants—short-lived desert plants that spend most of their lives as seeds. When it rains, the seeds sprout, flower, make seeds, and then die. Many desert wildflowers are ephemerals.

photosynthesis—the process of using the sun's energy to turn carbon dioxide and water into sugar.

stomata—small pores in a plant's leaves and stems that open to absorb carbon dioxide and release oxygen.

succulent—a type of plant that stores water in its fleshy leaves or stem. Cactuses, aloes, agaves, and euphorbias are all succulents.

transpiration—the process by which a plant loses water through stomata on its leaves and stems.

1998 UPDATE

TABLE OF CONTENTS

A Home Called Joshua

Objectives:
Understand the ways in which many kinds of desert animals depend on the same desert plant for food and/or shelter. Locate where on a Joshua tree different animals live or hunt.

Ages:
Intermediate

Materials:
- *Copies of pages 74 and 75*
- *Scissors*
- *Glue or tape*
- *Crayons or markers*

Subjects:
Science, Reading Comprehension

A desert is one of the harshest habitats on Earth in which to live. That goes for plants, animals, and humans. In the heat of the day, the cold of the night, and among many poisonous predators, desert animals must seek and find shelter if they are to stay alive. Challenge students to think of possible desert hideouts (under rocks, underground, in the shade of a cactus, in a rock crack, in a tree hole, etc.). The Joshua tree is a home for some and a place to hunt for others.

Joshua trees grow in the Mojave Desert in the southwestern United States (in parts of California, Nevada, Utah, and Arizona). It is the largest of the yuccas—desert evergreens that can grow 30 feet (9m) tall. Joshuas have spiny, knifelike, bluegreen leaves and whitish flowers.

Reproduce pages 74 and 75 and invite students to make their Joshua tree models (see below). Ask students to read "Life In A Joshua Tree" on the back of the model. Then, using the clues, locate each underlined animal, by lifting the flaps. Students should label each animal on the model. Focus attention on the column of desert animals students cut from page 74. Ask students to read the caption under each animal and, using the clues, decide where that animal goes on the outside of the model. Students can either cut out each animal and glue or tape it to the model or draw their own in the proper spot. Once again label each animal on the model. Invite students to color their models and to find out more about the creatures that live in or on a Joshua tree.

MAKING THE MODEL

1. Cut open the flaps on page 75 along the heavy black cut lines, then crease as shown.

2. Fold back the "Life in a Joshua Tree" along the fold line as shown:

3. Cut off the column of animals on page 74 along the cut line and set it aside:

4. Fit the remaining part of page 74 into folded page 75 as shown. Then turn the model around and tape the "Life in a Joshua Tree" panel to the back as shown:

Desert Duet

Compare the Sonoran and Sahara deserts

Objectives:
Create dioramas of the Sonoran and Sahara deserts. Identify plants and animals in each. Compare the two habitats for similarities and differences.

Ages:
Intermediate

Materials:
- *Copies of pages 76, 77, and 78*
- *Scissors*
- *Tape or glue*
- *Crayons or markers*

Subjects:
Science, Art, Writing Skills

Let your kids imagine that they have been hired by a natural history museum or a zoological conservation park to create exhibits of the Sonoran and Sahara deserts. The exhibits must identify desert plants and animals and provide information about each desert for museum goers or park visitors.

Challenge kids to obtain such information from the Deserts of the World insert in this book, as well as by referring to Grit, the Sand Grain, page 7; Desert Landforms, page 9; Animals of the Desert, pages 26–27; Community Squares, pages 40–41; and Desert Culture Day page 50. Encourage kids to find out the following about the Sonoran and the Sahara deserts: What kind of desert each is—high pressure, rain shadow, etc; how hot are they by day, how cool at night; annual rainfall amount; size; kinds of plants and animals; etc. Using this information challenge kids to write their own exhibit signs in the space provided on each sign piece. Allow kids to draw maps showing the location of each desert. Kids can also expand their dioramas by drawing other desert life or creating their own front piece or backdrop. You may wish to hand out the Copycat Desert Pictures on pages 76 and 77 for kids to cut out and incorporate into their scenes.

The curving front piece for each diorama is already labeled. For labeling the backdrops, read the following and have students find and label each plant and animal.

(continued on next page)

65

Sonoran Scene

Three pig-like *Javalinas* stand beside an *Octillo* tree with a *Vermillon Flycatcher* perched on it. Nearby a *Kit Fox* hears a *Rattlesnake* while a *Jackrabbit* eyes the fox ready to run to safety in an instant. A *Desert Tortoise* slowly crawls in front of a *Barrel Cactus*. Does it see *Harris' Hawk* flying above? On which of the four *Saguaro* cactuses is there a *Gila Woodpecker* and a *Hummingbird*? On which does a *Cactus Wren* sit? How many *Prickly Pear* cactuses can you find?

Sahara Scene

The oasis beneath the *Desert Palm* must look so inviting to the rider on the *Camel*. But the four *Barbary Sheep* could not care less. Nor the *Long-eared Desert Hedgehog* about to make a meal of a *Scarab Beetle*. Will a sudden desert storm cover the *Acacia Bush* with sand? *Lanner's Falcon* can fly off but what will happen to the *Skink* scurrying across the sand in search of shade? And will the *Sand Grouse* and her young make it to safety?

When the dioramas are complete, separate the class into groups and assign each one plant or animal to report on. Kids should research how their plant or animal is fitted, or adapted, to survive in the desert. Make a list of these adaptations on the board and compare those from the Sonoran desert to those from the Sahara.

Making the Dioramas

1. Color all the pictures.
2. Fold page 76 in half so the printed sides face out.
3. On page 77 cut out the Sonoran front piece, Gambel's quails, the Saguaro cactus with elf owl and Gila woodpecker, and the Sonoran sign piece.
4. Attach the left side of the front piece to the Sonoran background scene as shown:

tape fold behind

5. Attach the right side as shown:

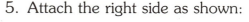

6. Tape or glue the quail and Saguaro cactus to the front or background scene wherever kids like.
7. Fill in the sign piece.
8. Fold and tape the sign as shown:

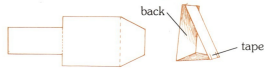

back

tape

9. Turn the diorama around and repeat for the Sahara scene. Tape or glue the Fennec fox and date palm wherever kids like.

Rain, Rain, Don't Go Away

Make a desert rain wheel to depict how the rainy season affects some desert life.

Objectives:
Understand how some desert life is adapted to take advantage of yearly heavy rainfall in order to complete their life cycles.

Ages:
Intermediate

Materials:
- **Copies of pages 81 and 82**
- **Scissors, glue**
- **Paper fasteners**
- **Lightweight cardboard**
- **Construction paper**
- **Crayons or markers**

Subject:
Science

Everyone has been thirsty at some time or another. But what is it like for plants and animals to live in a desert, where less than 10 inches (25 cm) of rain falls each year? And when it does finally rain, up to half the total yearly amount may fall during one thunderstorm?

If your students have ever lived through a dry spell, ask what happened to the plants in their backyards or in the park. Did a nearby pond dry up? If so, what happened to the pond plants and animals? How long did the spell extend before rain fell? Then what happened? Was the ground so dry that the water ran right off instead of soaking in? Did all of the backyard and park plants recover? What about the pond?

Review the ways in which many desert plants and animals are adapted to life without much rain. (See Plants of the Desert, pages 15-17, and Animals of the Desert, pages 26-27.) Ask kids what a cactus might look like after six or more rainless months. (It may be full of accordion-like folds.) Would they expect most woody desert plants to be full of leaves or nearly leafless? (Leafless–because by transpiration plants lose so much water through their leaves. Only deep-rooted desert plants that can reach underground water can keep their leaves year round.)

Invite kids to make their desert rain wheels. Ask them to turn the slot to read *Barrel Cactus.* By referring to the four pictures in the windows, challenge kids to describe orally or in writing how the cactus changes. For example, before the rain the barrel cactus appears shrunken and folded in. During the rain, its roots soak up all the water they can. Right after the rain, the cactus has swollen to store as much water as it can. Over the next few weeks, the cactus flowers and makes new seeds.

Have kids turn the wheel and compare the *Octillo* (oh-kuh-TEE-yoh), a woody desert plant, to the barrel cactus. Before the rain, the ocotillo is leafless. During the rain, its roots soak up water. After the rain, the tree leafs out. Finally the tree flowers and makes new seeds before shedding its leaves when dry season returns.

Before focusing on the *Spade-foot Toad,* make sure kids understand that it is an amphibian just like a frog. Amphibians spend the first part of their lives in water and the second on land, usually near enough to water that they can keep their skin moist.

Because of the shortage of water, desert spadefoot toads spend about eleven months of the year asleep in underground holes. When the rain awakens them, they dig out to feed, find mates, and lay eggs in pools of water left behind by the rain. In a day the eggs hatch into thousands of tadpoles that turn into toads in about two weeks. That is, unless the pools dry up first, killing the tadpoles before they can change into toads. After the rain, the toads hunt insects for a few weeks before digging themselves down into the soil for their long sleep.

Challenge kids to research what happens to fairy shrimp, green algae, and desert wildflowers before, during, and after the rain, then create their own circle of pictures to be fastened behind the circle with the four windows.

MAKING THE RAIN WHEEL

1. Color the pictures on page 80.
2. Glue page 80 to a piece of light-weight cardboard, then cut out the circle along the solid outer line only.
3. Glue page 79 to a piece of construction paper. Cut out the circle with the slot in it along the solid line.

4. Cut out the four windows on this circle.
5. Place the circle with the slot and windows on top of the circle on the cardboard. Push a paper fastener through the centers of both circles to join them.

Fossil Find

Locate fossils in the Gobi Desert

Objectives:
Learn about fossils found in the Gobi Desert and understand how they may have formed there.

Ages:
Primary

Materials:
- *Copies of pages 83 and 84*
- *Tape or glue*
- *Pencils, crayons, markers*

Subject:
Science

The Gobi is one of the world's most famous deserts. Not because it is located in northern China and southern Mongolia. Nor because it bakes in summer and freezes in winter. But because it was there in the 1920s, at a site called the Flaming Cliffs, that scientists from the American Museum of Natural History discovered many dinosaur fossils, including dinosaur eggs. These fossils dated back to the Late Cretaceous, the period before the dinosaurs became extinct about 65 million years ago.

Dinosaurs and other prehistoric creatures fascinate kids of all ages. Ask your kids to tell the class what they know about dinosaurs and fossils. Fossils are anything that remains of plants and animals that lived millions of years ago. They can be teeth, bones, shells, leaf outlines pressed into rock, footprints in hardened mud, or whole animals trapped in amber or frozen in soil.

When most living things die, their bodies are eaten or rot away completely. But if a plant or animal body is quickly buried in mud or sand where there is little oxygen, decay slows. While soft body parts do rot, harder bones, teeth, etc. can remain. Over time layers of mud or sand pile up on top of the buried remains and press on the mud and sand in which they are contained until that mud or sand hardens into rock. Inside the rock are the fossils. Everything that is known about dinosaurs comes from studying fossils. Scientists who study fossils are called paleontologists.

For over sixty years, the Soviet Union allowed only a few paleontologists to return to the Flaming Cliffs and other parts of the Gobi where fossils were found in the 1920s. With the fall of Communism, all that changed. In 1990 paleontologists from the American Museum returned to the Gobi. Not only did they dig around the Flaming Cliffs for new fossils, but they also explored other parts of the desert, including a place called Ukhaa Tolgod. Over the next few years the fossil finds of these scientists made headlines around the world, especially when they discovered new dinosaur species and even a dinosaur embryo.

Hand out copies of pages 81 and 82. Cut out both pictures along the solid black lines. Lay the Desert Dinosaur Dig picture under or next to the other picture. Turn them over and tape or glue them together. Turn the joined pictures back over. When all the kids have done, this read the following to them.

It is 80 million years ago. An Oviraptor sits on her nest full of eggs. She is ready to attack any egg eater with her jaws, claws, and powerful legs. Suddenly the wind picks up. There is thunder and rain. The wind grows stronger, lifts up a wall of sand and blows it at the dinosaur. In an instant she and her eggs are buried. They are trapped with no escape. For hours the sand piles up, thicker and thicker. When the storm is over, there is no sign of the dinosaur. Slowly the dead dinosaur's skin and soft body parts rot away. But her bones and some of her eggs' shells remain. For thousands of years the sand presses down on them as it hardens into sandstone. Inside the stone are the bones and shell. They are fossils.

Did this really happen millions of years ago? Perhaps. Now imagine you are a fossil scientist sent to the Gobi Desert. You spot what looks like a fossil in a rock. You dig and dig and find some of the Oviraptor's bones. You figure out where the bones belonged on the dinosaur's body and draw a picture. Some of the bones are still missing. Can you find them in the Dinosaur Dig picture? Circle them and draw a line from each to the place where you think it fits in the picture of the skeleton.

CAN YOU FIND THE MISSING BONES IN THE DESERT ROCKS?

Use the picture below to figure out where the missing bones fit into the Oviraptor's skeleton.

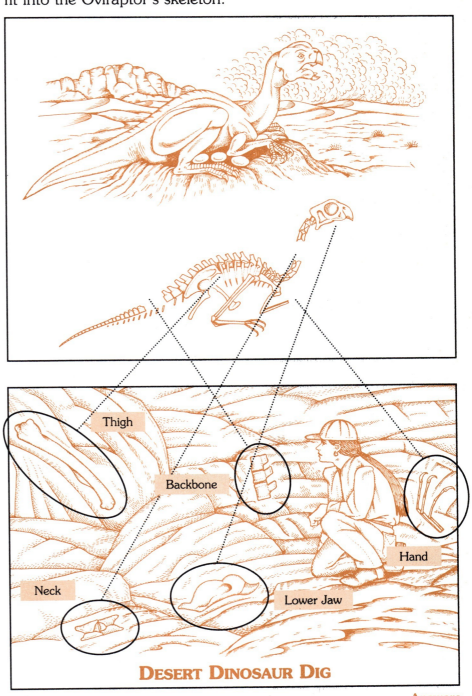

DESERT DINOSAUR DIG

Answers

Camel Rhebus, Camel Rama

Find out about the two kinds of camels.

Objectives:
To learn about camels and write a rhebus story about them using a camel diorama.

Ages:
First readers and reading challenged

Materials:
- *Copies of pages 85 and 86*
- *Scissors*
- *Tape or glue*
- *Pencils, crayons, markers*

Subjects:
Science, Reading, Writing, Art

RHEBUS KEY

CAMEL
NECK
TAIL
HUMP
DESERT
EYELASHES
NOSE or NOSTRILS
TOES
SAND or SAND
  DUNES
WATER
HUMP
HUMP
PLANTS or LEAVES
THORNS
BABY CAMEL
MILK
FIVE
SHIP
DESERT
PACKAGES
PERSON
HUMP
TWO HUMPS

I f there is one animal that kids associate with the word desert, it is the camel. Ask kids what they know about camels and list their responses on the board. Though some may contain incorrect information—such as that camels store water in their humps—do not correct what kids say. That can come later from the kids themselves.

Hand out copies of the camel rhebus on page 83. Go around the room and ask kids to read it aloud sentence by sentence replacing each picture with words. If you wish to tell kids a little more about camels, here are some facts they might enjoy.

CAMEL FUN FACTS

1. A camel with one hump is called a Dromedary. Two-humped camels are called Bactrian.
2. Camels feed on all kinds of desert plants. They eat thorny plants other desert animals don't. Like a cow, a camel swallows its food, then brings it up again to rechew.
3. Camels can go without water because they hardly sweat and lose little body water in urine or feces. When a thirsty camel finds water, it can drink 50 gallons at one time.
4. Spreading toes help a camel walk across sand in the same way that snowshoes help people walk over snow.
5. Camels can live up to 50 years. They form groups in which there may be thirty or so females, their young, and one male leader.
6. Camels have pads that protect their knees when they bend.
7. Dromedary camels live in the deserts of northern Africa and Arabia. Bactrian camels are found in the Gobi Desert in Asia. Bactrian camels grow longer, thicker hair than Dromedaries, which helps them survive in the cold Gobi.
8. If a camel can't find food, its hump will shrink and even lean to one side as the fat in it is used up.
9. Desert nomads depend on camels for transportation, as well as for milk and fleece. In return, the nomads take care of their camels and make sure these desert animals do not become extinct. (See Desert Culture Day, page 50, for more about people who live in the desert.)

Hand out copies of page 84 and invite kids to make a mini camel diorama. Allow them to arrange the camels any way they want and to draw a background scene or draw and cut out palms and tents that might be found at an oasis. Then hand out paper and challenge kids to write a short rhebus story about their scene. Let kids exchange rhebuses and read what their classmates wrote.

How To Make the Camel Rama

1. Take a piece of cardboard or oak tag that is 9×10 inches and tape rolls of tape or drop spots of glue down the middle as shown:

2. Place a piece of yellow construction paper on top of the cardboard so it touches the tape or glue down the middle. The yellow paper should hang over each end of the cardboard:

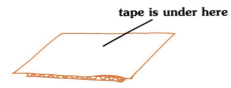

tape is under here

3. Lift and tape each overhanging end to the board as shown:

4. Cut out the three camels on page 84 along the heavy black line. Fold and crease the edges as shown:

5. Tape the camels together as shown:

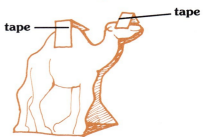

tape   tape

6. Cut out the nomad and fold in half as shown:

7. Fold the leg tab and tape as shown:

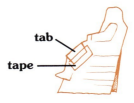

tab

tape

8. Place the nomad on top of a camel by spreading the blanket over the hump as shown:

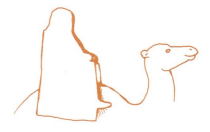

9. Arrange the camels on the wavy yellow dunes.

The Night of the Hunter

Make a field guide of predators that hunt the Sonoran Desert by night.

Objectives:
Learn how some desert predators are adapted to capture prey at night. Add entries to complete a field guide of night hunters.

Ages:
Intermediate

Materials:
- *Copies of pages 87, 88, and 89*
- *Scissors*
- *Stapler*
- *Crayons or markers*

Subjects:
Science and Art

s the sun slowly sinks below the horizon, its light is not the only thing that disappears from the desert. So does the day's scorching heat. Ask kids what happens to a hot pot of soup when the burner under it is turned off. (It cools.)

Does it cool faster or slower if the lid is left on (slower)? The desert is like the pot without the lid. For most of the year there are no clouds or moisture in the air to trap desert heat, so it escapes into space. Within a few hours of sundown, a desert can turn chilly, if not cold.

The cool night brings out hungry animals that hide from the sun by day. As darkness falls, kangaroo rats, pocket mice, crickets, beetles, jackrabbits, and other plant-eaters search for food. And wherever there are plant-eaters, there are predators.

Do the kids know of any animals that hunt at night? If so, how are these predators fitted, or adapted, to capture prey in near total darkness (keen eyesight in next to no light; heightened sense of hearing, smell, touch; movement that makes little noise; etc.)? If your kids were a hungry desert predator, how would they go about finding and capturing prey?

Photocopy pages 85, 86, and 87 and invite students to make their field guide of night hunters of the Sonoran Desert. Refer to the Deserts of the World insert after page 33 for information about the Sonoran.

Explain that a field guide is a book with the names and pictures of animals and/or plants that live in different places. There are field guides to reptiles, for instance, as well as guides to deserts. You may not own a field guide to deserts, but if you have one for reptiles, birds, or shells bring it in so kids can look at it. If not, try the library.

On the pages you hand out, there are pictures of eleven desert night hunters. Beneath seven of these is text for kids to read. Encourage kids to express their feelings about the animals and the ways they hunt. Point out that predators do not kill for fun; they kill prey for food. Focus on the venomous hunters and explain that venom is a poison that is injected through a bite or sting. Tarantulas and wolf spiders have very mild venoms, but that of a rattlesnake is usually deadly. A human bitten by a rattlesnake is in danger of dying if not treated promptly. Ask kids why they should avoid all venomous animals if they ever explore a desert. In addition to stressing that kids must always be careful not to be bitten or stung, be sure to reinforce the idea that no animal should be disturbed or harmed, even if that animal poses little threat to humans.

Using the text under the seven pictures as a model, kids should consult books and research similar kinds of

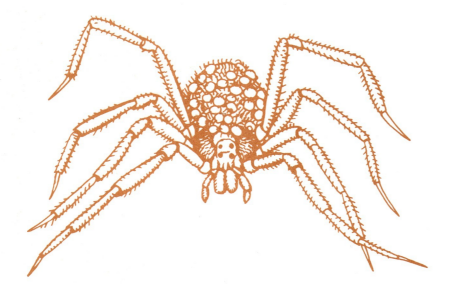

facts to fill in the entries under the remaining four pictures. For instance, how is a kingsnake like a rattlesnake? How are they different? You may have to provide kids with library books or field guides about deserts, night hunters, etc. or allow them library access to complete their research. Invite kids to read their entries. Why would they think a field guide is a necessity for desert visitors? (It tells which animals bite or sting, how to identify them, how to avoid them, where they may be hiding by day, how to identify plants, etc.)

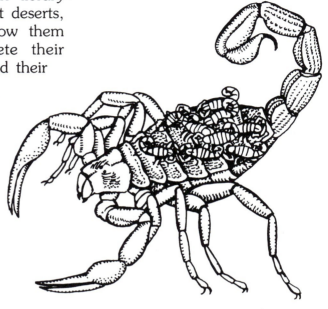

MAKING THE FIELD GUIDE

1. Fold each page in half along the middle solid line, then in half again so the printed sides are on the outside.
2. Nest the three folded pages together so that the numbers are in order from the cover to 12. Pages 6 and 7 should be in the center. Pages 8 to 12 have neither picture nor printed text.
3. Staple the folded sheets in the middle as shown:

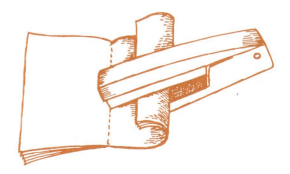

The Desert Night Snake slithers up the Joshua's trunk in search of lizards to eat.

At the edge of a high branch, Scott's Oriole rests, sings, and feeds on insects.

cut line

The Cactus Wren guards the tube-like nest she built of Joshua leaves.

On the ground, the Desert Night Lizard hunts for tasty termites in dead wood.

The Wood Rat brings nearly everything it finds back to its nest at the base of the Joshua tree. The nest is a mound of fallen leaves.

LIFE IN A JOSHUA TREE

The Joshua tree is many things to many desert creatures. To the *Gila Woodpecker* hiding in a tree hole, it is a cool spot to sit on her nestful of eggs. To the baby *Cactus Wren* tucked in the nest its mother built, the Joshua is a safe place to hatch from its egg. Near the tip of a branch a *spider and a pseudoscorpion* hunt for insects that live under tree bark. You'll find some of these *insects* not far from the ground in the tree's trunk. When a branch dies, *termites* may feed on dead fallen wood. These insects attract lizards and other termite eaters. On the ground nearby, a *Desert Shrew* moves in to share a *Wood Rat's* nest of fallen leaves. One juicy beetle will provide the shrew with both food and water. Look for a big bunch of flowers at the end of a tree branch. That's where you will also find a *Yucca Moth*. By carrying pollen, the moth helps the flowers make seeds. But in the pollen the moth lays eggs. When the eggs hatch, the tiny caterpillars find enough seeds to eat so they can grow and turn into moths. One of the uneaten seeds may become a new Joshua tree.

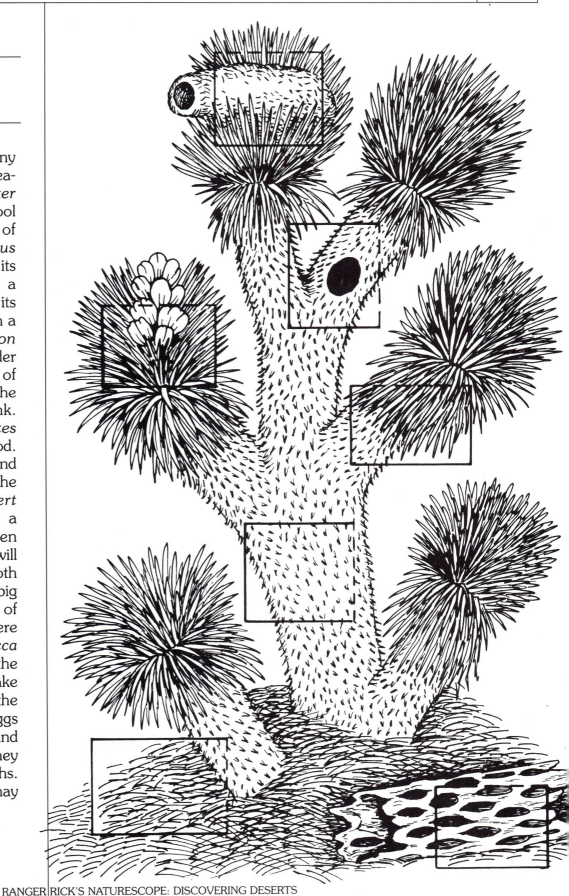

DESERT DUET

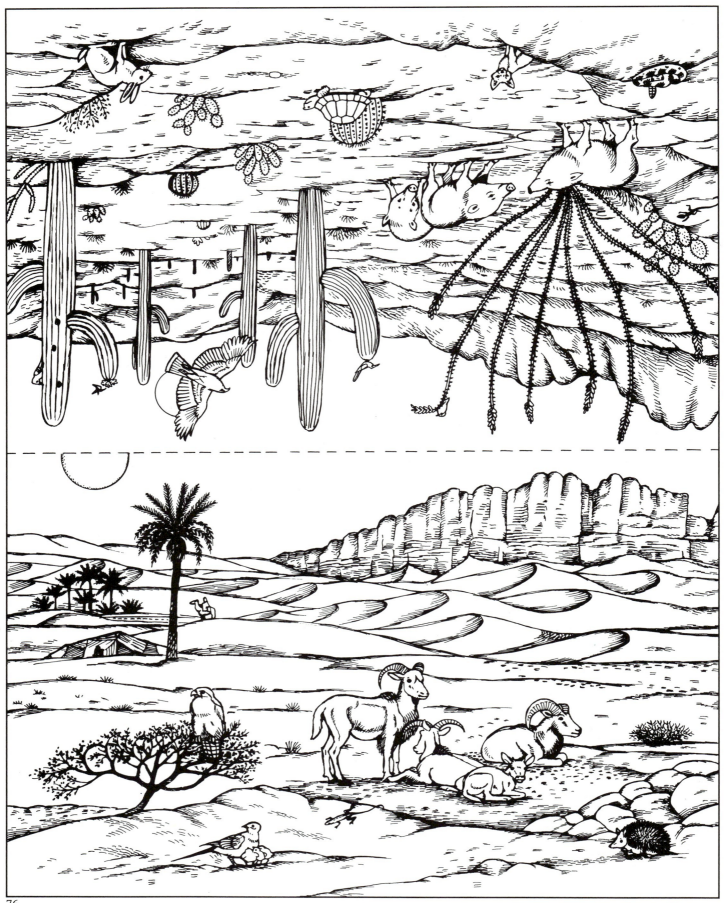

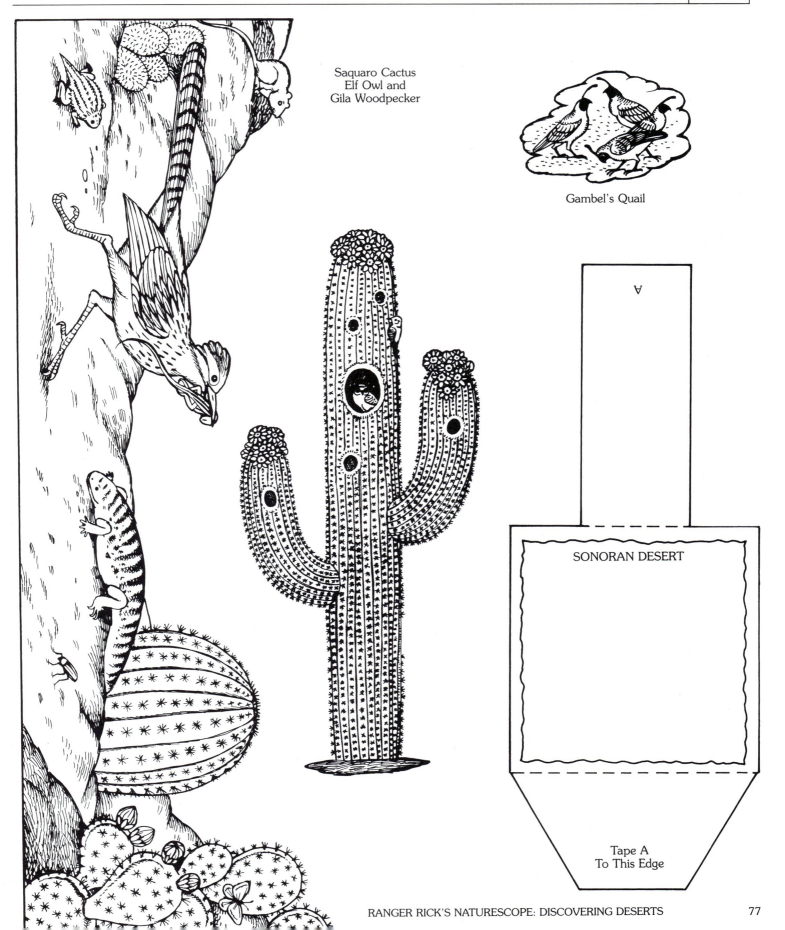

Saquaro Cactus
Elf Owl and
Gila Woodpecker

Gambel's Quail

A

SONORAN DESERT

Tape A
To This Edge

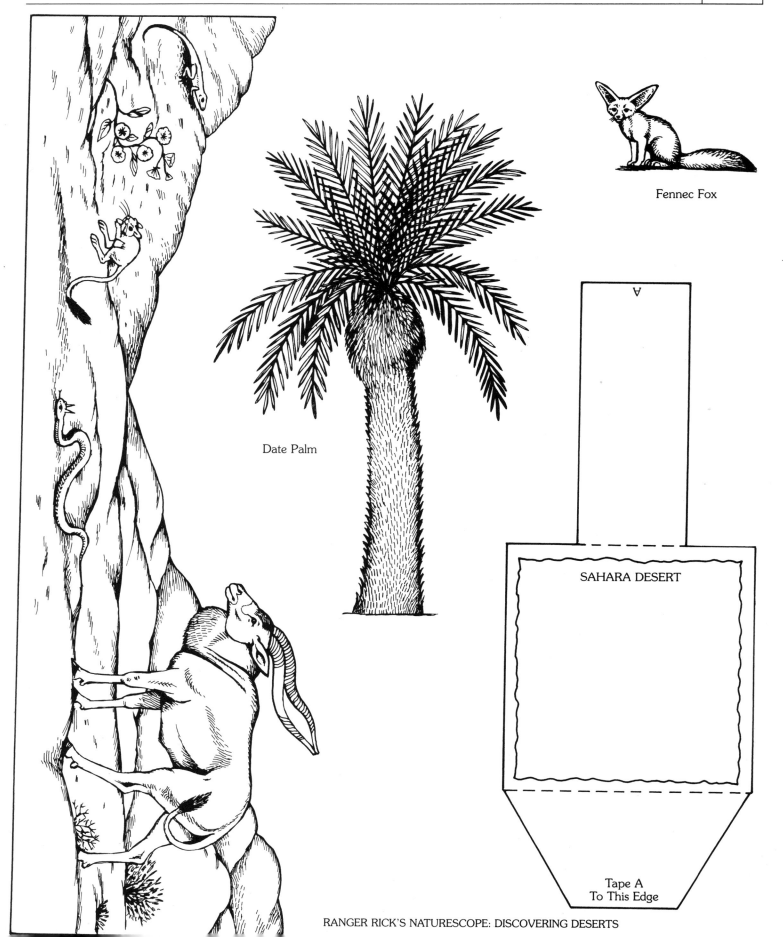

Fennec Fox

Date Palm

A

SAHARA DESERT

Tape A
To This Edge

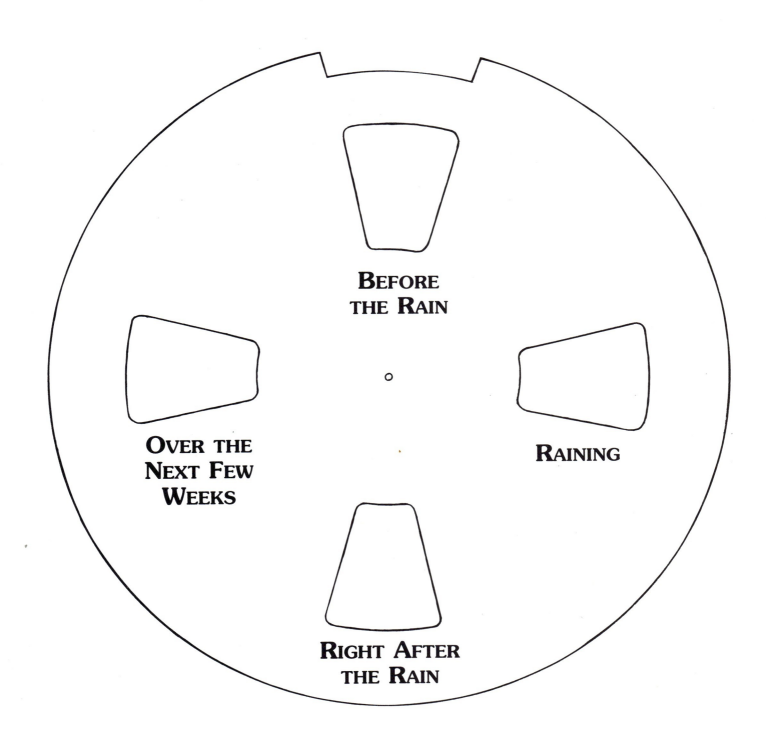

BEFORE
THE RAIN

OVER THE
NEXT FEW
WEEKS

RAINING

RIGHT AFTER
THE RAIN

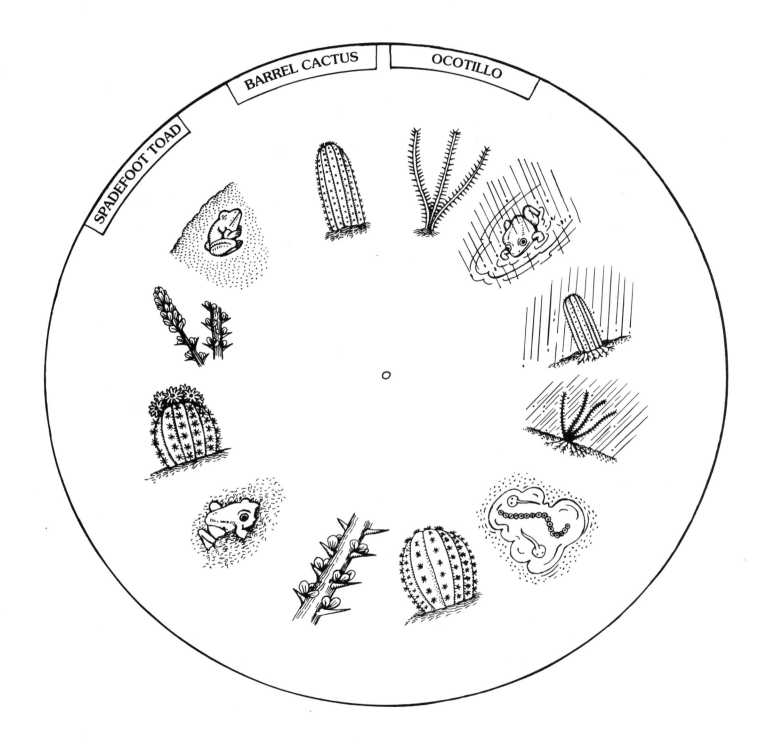

DESERT DINOSAUR DIG

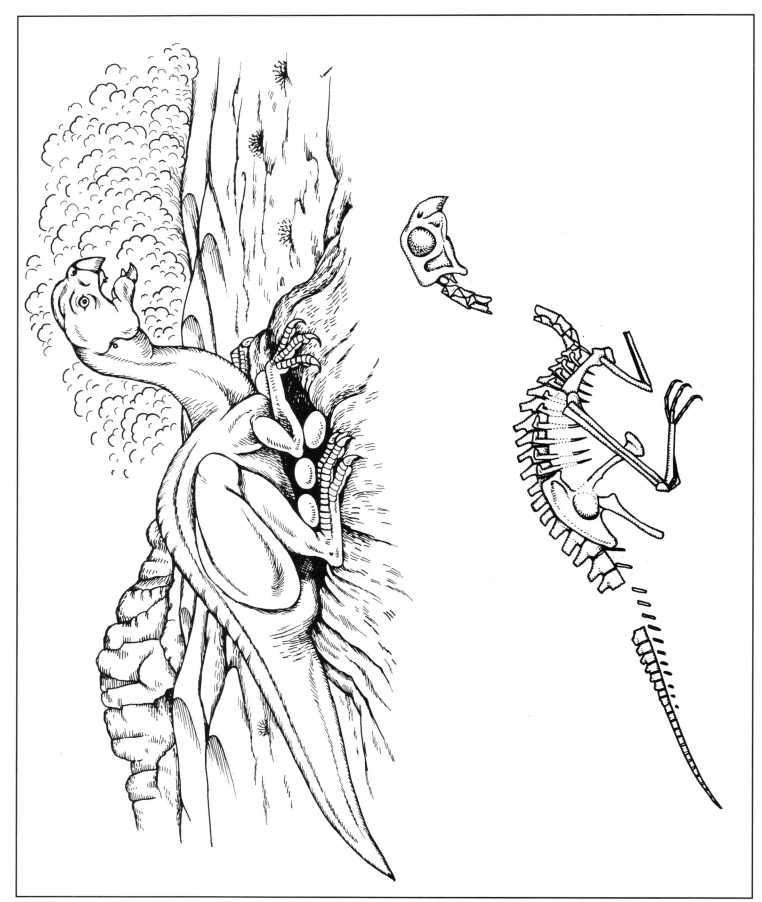

The Camel

Come meet a

It has a long , a  , and a

It lives in the  where there is lots of sand.

A camel's long  help keep sand out of its eyes.

A camel's  can close to keep sand out of it.

A camel's  spread so it can walk easily across

A camel can go a long time with very little

But it does not store water in its

The is full of fat.

A camel lives off the fat when it can't find  to eat.

A baby 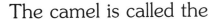 gets food and water from its mother's

It grows to full size by the time it is 5 years old.

The camel is called the  of the

Why? Because it can carry so many  or a

There are only two kinds of camel.

One kind has one and the other kind has

83

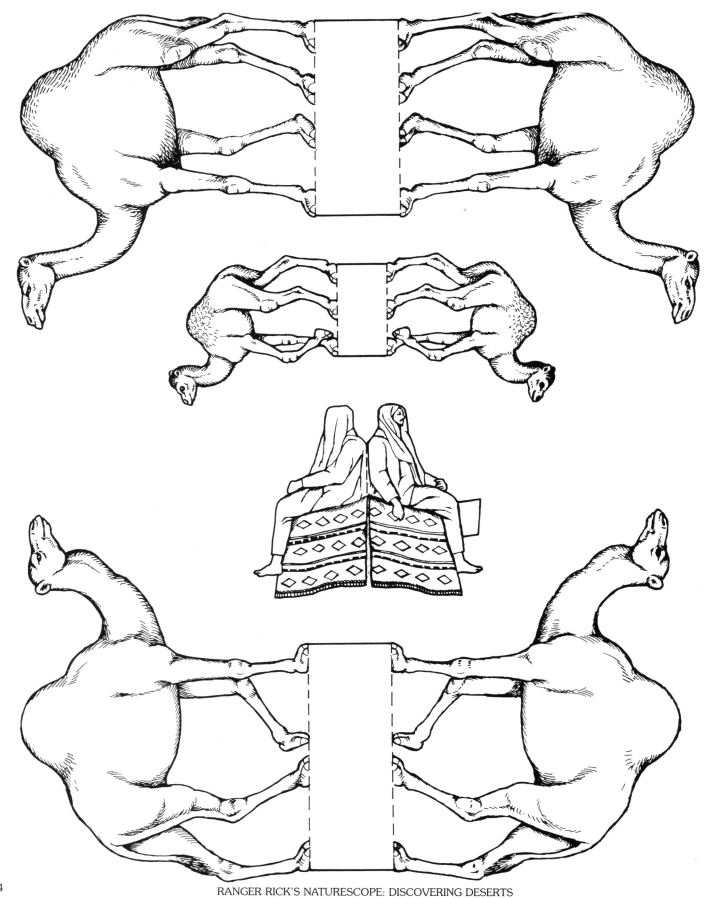

DESERT NIGHT HUNTERS

1

KIT FOX

12

2

BLACK WIDOW SPIDER

With their biting fangs, all spiders can inject venom into insects and other prey to keep them from moving. But the venom of the black widow spider is one of the deadliest. It can make people sick. Unlike insects, spiders and scorpions have eight legs, not six.

11

KING SNAKE

_____

_____

_____

_____

_____

TARANTULA

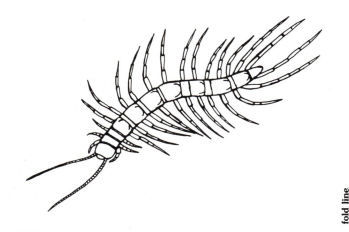

GIANT CENTIPEDE

Need a good reason not to turn over a desert rock? A giant centipede may be hiding under it. And its bite can be very painful. This many-legged night hunter can grow 10 inches (25 cm) long.

3

fold line

fold line

10

4

9

BOBCAT

Jackrabbits and gophers, beware! A bobcat may be hiding nearby ready to pounce. If you escape, the cat will chase you at full speed. You must avoid the cat's sharp claws and powerful bite. Bobcats grow about twice as big as most house cats.

WOLF SPIDER

_____

_____

_____

_____

_____